HELP PULL-DOWN MENU

<u>Help</u>
<u>C</u>ontents
<u>S</u>earch for Help on...
<u>H</u>ow to Use Help
<u>W</u>indows Tutorial
<u>A</u>bout Program Manager...

D1507464

DOCUMENT CONTROL MENU

<u>R</u>estore	
<u>M</u>ove	
<u>S</u>ize	
Mi<u>n</u>imize	
Ma<u>x</u>imize	
<u>C</u>lose	Ctrl+F4
Ne<u>x</u>t	Ctrl+F6

TASK LIST WINDOW

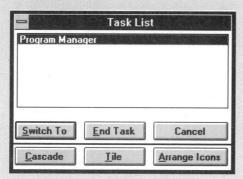

Task List
Program Manager

Switch To	End Task	Cancel
Cascade	Tile	Arrange Icons

Computer users are not all alike. Neither are SYBEX books.

We know our customers have a variety of needs. They've told us so. And because we've listened, we've developed several distinct types of books to meet the needs of each of our customers. What are you looking for in computer help?

If you're looking for the basics, try the **ABC's** series. You'll find short, unintimidating tutorials and helpful illustrations. For a more visual approach, select **Teach Yourself**, featuring screen-by-screen illustrations of how to use your latest software purchase.

Mastering and **Understanding** titles offer you a step-by-step introduction, plus an in-depth examination of intermediate-level features, to use as you progress.

Our **Up & Running** series is designed for computer-literate consumers who want a no-nonsense overview of new programs. Just 20 basic lessons, and you're on your way.

We also publish two types of reference books. Our **Instant References** provide quick access to each of a program's commands and functions. SYBEX **Encyclopedias** and **Desktop References** provide a *comprehensive reference* and explanation of all of the commands, features, and functions of the subject software.

Sometimes a subject requires a special treatment that our standard series don't provide. So you'll find we have titles like **Advanced Techniques, Handbooks, Tips & Tricks,** and others that are specifically tailored to satisfy a unique need.

We carefully select our authors for their in-depth understanding of the software they're writing about, as well as their ability to write clearly and communicate effectively. Each manuscript is thoroughly reviewed by our technical staff to ensure its complete accuracy. Our production department makes sure it's easy to use. All of this adds up to the highest quality books available, consistently appearing on best-seller charts worldwide.

You'll find SYBEX publishes a variety of books on every popular software package. Looking for computer help? Help Yourself to SYBEX.

For a complete catalog of our publications:

SYBEX Inc.
2021 Challenger Drive, Alameda, CA 94501
Tel: (510) 523-8233/(800) 227-2346 Telex: 336311
Fax: (510) 523-2373

SYBEX is committed to using natural resources wisely to preserve and improve our environment. As a leader in the computer book publishing industry, we are aware that over 40% of America's solid waste is paper. This is why we have been printing the text of books like this one on recycled paper since 1982.

This year our use of recycled paper will result in the saving of more than 15,300 trees. We will lower air pollution effluents by 54,000 pounds, save 6,300,000 gallons of water, and reduce landfill by 2,700 cubic yards.

In choosing a SYBEX book you are not only making a choice for the best in skills and information, you are also choosing to enhance the quality of life for all of us.

The ABC's of Windows 3.1

the
abc's
SERIES

The ABC's of Windows™ 3.1

BY ALAN R. NEIBAUER

SYBEX ®

San Francisco
Paris
Düsseldorf
Soest

ACQUISITIONS EDITOR: *Dianne King*

DEVELOPMENTAL EDITOR: *Christian Crumlish*

EDITOR: *Kayla Sussell*

TECHNICAL EDITOR: *Lillian Chen*

WORD PROCESSORS: *Ann Dunn and Susan Trybull*

BOOK DESIGNER: *Amparo Del Rio*

CHAPTER ART AND LAYOUT: *Helen Bruno*

SCREEN GRAPHICS: *Cuong Le and Richard Green*

TYPESETTER: *Elizabeth Newman*

PROOFREADER/PRODUCTION ASSISTANT: *Lisa Haden*

INDEXER: *Anne Leach*

COVER DESIGNER: *Ingalls + Associates*

COVER PHOTOGRAPHER: *David Bishop*

Library of Congress Card Number: 91-67907

ISBN: 0-89588-839-4

Manufactured in the United States of America

10 9 8 7 6 5

To Barbara

A C K N O W L E D G M E N T S

Although only my name is on the cover of this book, a dedicated group of professionals at Sybex deserve much of the credit. Even though Windows is an easy program to use, working with it through all of its developmental cycles presented challenges requiring the talents of many individuals. Without their help and support this book would not be a reality.

Christian Crumlish served as developmental editor. It was his responsibility to organize the overall effort, and to keep everyone on time.

The day-to-day responsibilities for seeing this book into print rested with the copy editor, Kayla Sussell. She sustained it during all of the revisions, rewrites, and changes in the software that often sent us back to page one.

My special thanks go to technical editor, Lillian Chen. Maintaining the technical accuracy of a book is always a difficult task. It was even more difficult because of the complex nature of Windows' development cycle.

Also, my thanks to proofreader Lisa Haden, typesetter Elizabeth Newman, word processors Ann Dunn and Susan Trybull, indexer Anne Leach, and chapter designer Helen Bruno. You may not see their names on the covers of Sybex books, but you do see the excellent quality of their work.

My appreciation also goes to Joanne Cuthbertson, Barbara Gordon, and Dianne King.

I especially want to thank all of those at Sybex who maintained their courage during some trying times. It is unimaginably difficult to perform professionally while fires rage and homes are destroyed. They have my respect and admiration.

Finally, my thanks to Barbara Neibauer, whom I was lucky enough to marry 25 years ago. She is my friend, advisor, and therapist. I am warmed by the joy I see in her eyes and the infinite depth of her heart.

Contents AT A GLANCE

Table of Contents

PART THREE The File Manager

PART FOUR   The Accessories

PART FIVE   Specialty Tasks

PART SIX Customizing Windows

APPENDICES

icrosoft, the company that developed DOS, the world's most popular operating system, has again revolutionized the PC world with Windows. In the past few years, Windows has evolved from being an interesting, although limited graphic environment, to the extraordinarily powerful platform that it is today. If you are familiar only with the Windows of some years ago, you will be amazed by the versatility and power of Windows today. Windows not only turns the computer into a more efficient and productive tool, it is also easy and fun to use. The dream of the PC pioneers, who envisioned a day when everyone could use a personal computer effectively, is now a reality.

Version 3.1 of Windows, which this book describes, includes features that even the inventors of the PC did not foresee. It includes, for example, TrueType—a system of quality scalable fonts that can be used on any Windows-supported printer. Now you don't have to struggle with third-party printer fonts to produce publication-quality documents. With TrueType, you can print your documents from the office laser printer or from your home dot-matrix printer without qualms about the quality of the finished product.

If you are just learning how to use Windows, then this book is ideal for you because it is arranged in short, easy-to-follow lessons. Each lesson will take only a few minutes to follow but will guide you through a complete and useful task. Because the lessons are *task oriented*, you will be able to apply them immediately to your own work, without having to read additional lessons or reference materials. You may even be able to master several lessons in one session to build your Windows skills quickly and painlessly.

How to Use this Book

If you just purchased Windows, the two appendices will be invaluable. In Appendix A, you will learn how to copy your disks, and how to install Windows on your computer. If you have not yet installed Windows, go directly to this appendix.

Appendix B discusses how to install additional printers and screen and printer fonts. After you become accustomed to working with Windows, use Appendix B if you want to customize your printer and fonts to match your specific needs.

In Part 1, "Learning about Windows," you will learn about Program Manager, the program that controls the overall Windows environment. You will also learn how to start Windows and how to interact with its menus and dialog boxes to perform Windows' powerful functions efficiently. In addition, you will learn how to access on-line help for Windows features and commands.

In Part 2, "Working with Windows," the lessons explain how to use Windows to increase your efficiency and productivity. You will learn how to run your application programs, and how to use the windows from which Windows takes its name. A window is an independent area of the screen in which Windows displays an application, document, or other information. You can divide the screen into multiple windows so that you can work with more than one application at a time, switching back and forth between them.

Part 3 is devoted completely to lessons about File Manager. File Manager is the Windows program that allows you to work with disks, directories, and files. You will learn how to change disks and subdirectories; how to work with directory trees and program listings; and how to run programs using alternative methods. You will also learn how to copy, move, rename, and delete files and directories, and how to copy and format floppy diskettes.

Windows desktop accessories are discussed in Part 4. These accessories provide electronic versions of the important tools you use every day, including a clock, calculator, calendar, card file, and notepad. By running accessories in windows on your screen, these important tools become available at the click of a mouse or the touch of a key. In Part 4 you will also learn about Terminal, a communication program that links your computer with the world through a modem; Write, an easy-to-use word processing program; and Paintbrush, a drawing program for creating presentation-quality artwork.

Part 5 discusses special tasks which you will find useful for a variety of jobs. You will learn how to share text and graphics between applications, and how to print files quickly—even those from diverse applications—from within File Manager. You will also learn how to organize your files in groups and how to return temporarily to the DOS prompt to perform that rare function not suitable for Windows.

Finally, after reading Part 6, you will be able to customize Windows to your own personal taste. You will learn how to control the speed of Windows' response to the mouse and keyboard; to adjust the overall look of the Windows screen; to control multimedia equipment and warning beeps; and to set the date and time of your computer's clock.

FOLLOWING THE INSTRUCTIONS IN THIS BOOK

Many lessons in this book guide you step-by-step through specific tasks. Just follow each instruction to master the procedure being discussed. You will see several different types of instruction. Here are a few rules to follow to help you differentiate between this book's instructions, your typed input, and what Windows displays on the screen:

- When you are told to do something on the computer, you will be given a series of numbered steps to follow, such as:

  1. Type **CD**.
  2. Press ↵.
  3. Type **WIN** and press ↵.

- When you are asked to type something using the keyboard, what must be typed will appear in boldface, as above: Type **CD**.

- When Windows displays a message on-screen in response to an action you have performed, the information will appear like this:

This will end your Windows session.

Read all of the information in the step before performing it. In some cases, a step may include optional instructions for mouse and keyboard users even though most of the instructions in this book are written for mouse users. However, even when you are using a mouse, you may find some of the keyboard instructions more efficient.

In a few instances, you will see a series of steps that give general rather than specific instructions. These are designed as aids to follow when you are performing your own work—you need not do them to complete the lesson and the text will indicate this.

Mouse Techniques

If you have a mouse, you will see a symbol on your screen called the *pointer*. This indicates the position of your mouse. The shape of the pointer will depend on its location on the screen. When an instruction says to *point to* something on the screen, move the mouse on your desk until the pointer is on top of the object on the screen.

An instruction to *click* the mouse means to quickly press and release the left mouse button. If an instruction says

Click on the box

it means to point to the box referred to in the text and to click the left mouse button.

The instruction to *double-click* means to perform two clicks rapidly without pausing. The speed with which you must click the mouse depends on your system. If you double-click to follow an instruction and nothing happens, then you did not click fast enough—try again.

The instruction *to drag* means to point to an object, press and *hold down* the left mouse button, and then while holding down the button, to move the mouse on your desk. Instructions to drag always tell you where to drag to, as in

Drag the pointer to the bottom of the screen

When you reach the destination, then you release the mouse button.

If You Do Not Have a Mouse

Although a mouse isn't absolutely necessary for using Windows, it is highly recommended. Without a mouse, you lose much of the ease of use and flexibility for which Windows was designed. So most of the instructions in this book instruct you to perform Windows functions with a mouse.

You will find, however, in the first few lessons that we've given the equivalent keyboard instructions for mouse commands. This will make it easier for you to use Windows if you do not have a mouse yet. In addition, there are three useful tables of keystrokes for navigating through File Manager, Program Manager, and all dialog boxes on the inside covers. Beyond the initial lessons and the back covers, the instructions are mainly for mouse users.

Many mouse commands, however, have equivalent *shortcut keystrokes*. These are one or two keystrokes that perform the same function as selecting options from a menu or dialog box with the mouse. If you do not have a mouse, using the shortcut keys can save you many unnecessary keystrokes. Even when you are using a mouse, you may find these shortcut keys to be very efficient, particularly if you are typing at the keyboard and do not want to move your hands to use the mouse. These shortcut keystrokes are shown inside parentheses after the mouse instructions, as in:

To exit Windows, double-click on Program Manager's control box (Alt-F4).

This means that you can exit Windows either by following the mouse instruction to double-click, or by pressing Alt-F4, holding down the Alt key and simultaneously pressing the F4 function key.

Finally, the more you use Windows, the more you will discover about it. Take your time to master each skill before going on to the next one. If you must look ahead to perform some important task, be sure to return to the lesson where you left off because the book is arranged in such a way that you will build on previously acquired knowledge, step-by-step.

Windows will be an invaluable tool for you. I hope you enjoy using it and becoming a part of this new era in computing.

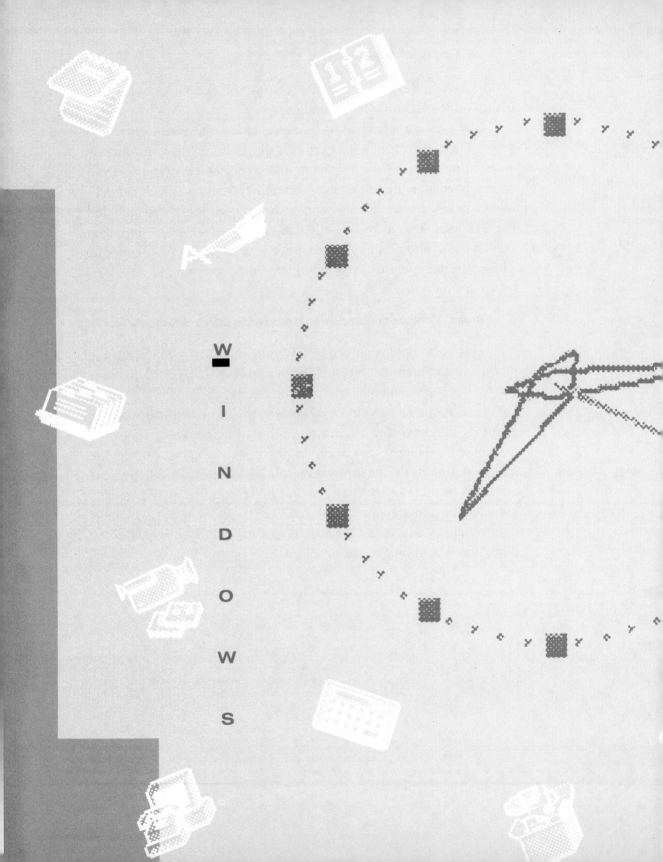

PART 1

Learning about Windows

Windows 3.1 is an extremely powerful, multifeatured program. In spite of its power, it is remarkably easy to use because of its user-friendly interface. Using Windows, you will be able to work with all of your applications and documents effectively and efficiently once you master a few basic skills.

In Lessons 1 through 6, you will learn about the many benefits that Windows offers and how to communicate with its graphic interface. You will also learn how to get on-line help for all of Windows' features.

If you have not already done so, carefully follow the instructions in Appendix A to install Windows on your computer. Then, beginning with Lesson 1, use this book to learn how to use Windows and how to communicate with it.

Introducing
Windows 3.1

asically, the computer component of your computer system is a series of electronic circuits. Therefore, in order to communicate with it, you need an input device such as a keyboard or mouse, and an output device such as a monitor or printer.

All communications between a computer and its input and output devices are controlled by an operating system. Most personal computers use DOS as their operating systems. When you start up your computer, DOS is loaded into the computer's memory and it is always ready to interpret your commands to the computer system. For example, when you type **dir** and press ↵, DOS interprets the command and displays the current directory or listing of the files in the current directory on your disk drive. Without the operating system acting as an interface, there would be no way to communicate with your computer's electronic circuits.

But the user interface with DOS is not perfect. All that you will see on the screen when you start DOS is the prompt C>. You must memorize all of the DOS commands, and know the correct syntax for entering them if you want DOS to be able to follow your instructions.

Most programs designed to work with DOS have their own sets of commands. How you would print a file from WordPerfect for DOS, for example, is not how you would print a file from WordStar or Microsoft Word for DOS. So, you must learn a complete new set of commands for every DOS program that you install on your computer.

In addition, most DOS programs have their own specific ways of dealing with printers and monitors, so you must go through a separate installation process for each program, configuring it to work with your hardware. Just because your word processor works with your printer, there is no guarantee that you'll be able to print spreadsheets.

Windows is designed to solve these somewhat intimidating problems, and to ensure that the printing process runs smoothly.

Windows Replaces the DOS Interface

Windows is not an operating system: in fact, it requires you to have DOS already installed on your computer in order to run. Windows *replaces* the DOS *interface*, and changes the way in which you communicate with your computer to give commands and work with your application programs. Even more than this, Windows provides an interactive environment, which means that when you are using your computer, you are engaged in a continuous "dialog" with the system.

Windows is a graphical user interface (GUI). This means that the commands that you'll want to perform will be displayed on the screen. For example, instead of having to remember (or look up) specific DOS commands, you select the operation that you want to perform from the menu choices that are displayed. (See Figure 1.1.)

The GUI also makes it easy to work with disks and directories. It can display a tree-like diagram of the directories on your hard disk, which shows the relationship between the directories and the subdirectories that they contain. (See Figure 1.2.) You can display directory listings, change directories, and run programs using the point-and-click method.

This method is used to perform most operations. To "point and click" means that you place the mouse pointer on the name of the function and then click the left mouse button. Windows will prompt you each step of the way until the operation is completed.

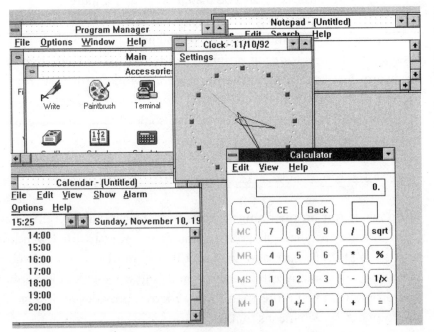

FIGURE 1.1:

Windows is a graphical user interface that displays options and functions on-screen.

Windows takes its name from the on-screen "windows" that it uses to display information. A window is an area of the screen that Windows sets aside for a specific task. You can run several programs at the same time, each in its own window. You can choose to have one program's window occupy the entire screen to display as much information as is possible, or to display all windows simultaneously, as shown in Figure 1.3. The windows can also be hidden in the background while you work with one program in the foreground.

Windows and Your Application Programs

When you install Windows on your computer system, you configure it to work with your monitor, printer, and other hardware. This installation process sets the environment under which all Windows applications can operate. A *Windows application* is a program, such as Excel or WordPerfect for Windows, that has been designed specifically to work with Windows and which cannot be run without first running Windows.

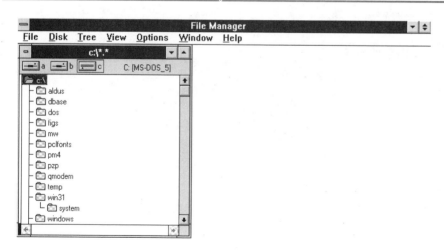

FIGURE 1.2:

Windows File Manager uses tree diagrams to graphically represent the directory structure.

When you install a Windows application, you do not have to configure it for your hardware because it automatically uses the hardware recognized by Windows itself. For example, if you install Windows to work with your printer, *every* Windows application will work with your printer automatically.

In addition, all Windows applications share a common set of commands. For example, you open, save, and print files the same way with all Windows applications. You do not have to learn different commands for each of them. *All* Windows applications can be run full-screen or in their own smaller windows, sharing the screen with other applications.

Furthermore, you can run non-Windows applications (called DOS applications) under Windows using the point-and-click method. Each DOS application must be installed separately, however, and configured for your hardware as explained in the application's manual. The hardware information that you installed with Windows cannot be used with DOS applications. With all computer systems, you can run DOS

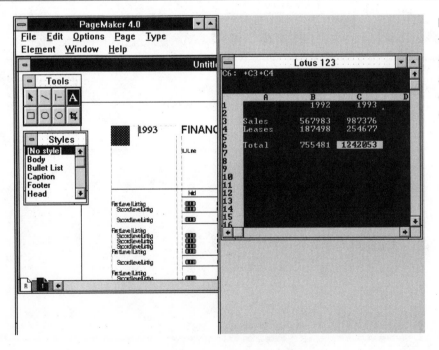

FIGURE 1.3:

You can run more than one program at a time, each displayed in its own window.

applications full-screen. If you have a 386 type of processor (CPU) or higher, with enough memory, you can also run DOS applications in their own windows. Figure 1.3, for example, shows PageMaker, which is a Windows application, and a DOS version of Lotus 1-2-3 running in their own windows at the same time. If you do not have sufficient memory to run both applications in their own windows, you can still run Lotus 1-2-3 full-screen while PageMaker waits to be called up in the background.

Of course, you can always exit Windows to run DOS applications from the DOS prompt.

WINDOWS ALLOWS YOU TO SHARE DATA

Whether you run two applications separately or at the same time, you can share data between them easily by using the Windows Clipboard. The Clipboard is an area in your computer's memory where Windows temporarily stores copied data. The Clipboard can be used to copy both text and graphics, as shown in Figure 1.4. Here, a drawing created with

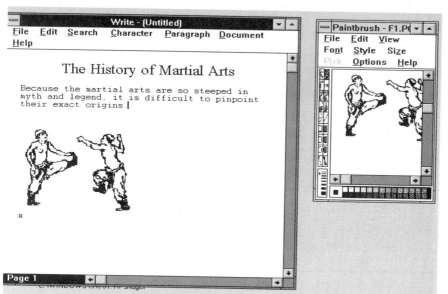

FIGURE 1.4:

Windows allows you to share information between applications using the Clipboard.

Paintbrush (a powerful drawing tool, provided with Windows), was copied to a document created with Write, which is Windows' word processing program. If you want to include a spreadsheet in a report, you would copy the data into the Clipboard, display the report in the Write window, and then paste the data in place.

What You Need to Run Windows

Note that Windows isn't perfect either. To run several large applications at the same time requires a lot of memory. Also, Windows can be difficult to set up and configure, especially on systems with special memory requirements or with unique combinations of hardware and software. Nevertheless, once you have set up and configured Windows, you will be able to run Windows applications effortlessly.

To run Windows you need the following components:

- an IBM-PC AT or compatible computer

- a hard disk drive with 6 to 8MB of free space

- at least one floppy drive

- at least 1MB of memory (2MB or more is preferred)

- a Windows-compatible monitor and graphics adaptor

- DOS version 3.1 or higher

- a mouse (optional, but *highly* recommended)

Strictly speaking you don't *need* a printer to run Windows, but you will want to get a Windows-compatible printer too. It is also useful, but optional, to have extended or expanded memory to speed up Windows operations.

The type of computer and the amount of memory you have, determine the type and number of programs that you can run simultaneously. You'll learn more about this in Lesson 2 where you will learn how to start Windows.

FEATURING

Starting
Windows
automatically

Starting
Windows in
operation mode

▼

Starting Windows

Now that you have some idea of how useful Windows will be to you, you are ready to start it. Make sure that you have installed Windows by following either the instructions that came with it or those in Appendix A of this book. Once Windows has been installed, follow these steps.

1. Start your computer.

Respond to the date and time prompts if they appear. Type the date in MM-DD-YY format, such as 10-11-92, and press ↵. Then type the time in HH:SS format, such as 10:16, and press ↵. If it is past noon, use military time by adding 12 to the hours. For example, if it is 2:30 p.m., enter 14:30. If your computer is already on and you just installed Windows for the first time, press Ctrl-Alt-Del. (Be sure to press all three keys at the same time.) This will restart your computer and load into memory any configuration information that the installation process may have added to your system.

2. Type **WIN** and press ↵.

As Windows loads itself into your computer's memory, the Windows logo will appear for a few moments. You will then see the initial Windows screen appear with the Program Manager window and the Main Group window open. (See Figure 2.1.) The small pictures that you see on the screen are called *icons*. These are graphic representations of

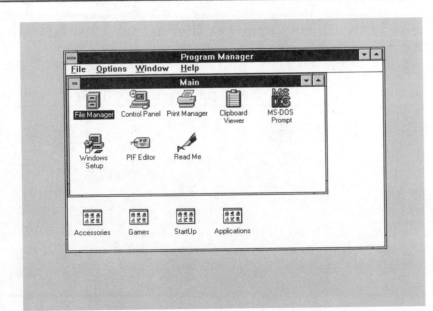

FIGURE 2.1:

The initial Windows screen looks like this.

the different Windows programs that you will be using. Program Manager is the Windows application that you'll use to run programs and to organize your programs and documents into groups. Also, when you want to quit Windows to go to DOS, you can exit Windows only from Program Manager. Note that your screen may differ from Figure 2.1 depending on your hardware and how Windows was installed.

If Windows starts correctly, and in the future you want to continue using the procedure that you just learned to start Windows, then move on to Lesson 3. If the Windows screen does not appear, or if you want Windows to start automatically whenever you turn on your computer, then continue with this lesson until you have finished it.

How to Start Windows Automatically

If you plan to use Windows every time you start up your computer, and you want it to start automatically, follow these steps:

1. Type **CD** and then press ↵ to change to the root directory.

2. Type **COPY AUTOEXEC.BAT + CON: AUTOEXEC.BAT** and press ↵. You will see

> **AUTOEXEC.BAT**
> **CON**

on the screen.

3. Type **WIN** and press ↵.

4. Press Ctrl-Z.
The characters ^Z will appear.

5. Press ↵.

Now, Windows will start automatically whenever you start your computer, or whenever you restart it using Ctrl-Alt-Del.

What to Do If Windows Does Not Start

If you try to start Windows and do not see the initial screen, but you get the error message

Bad command or file name

that means that DOS cannot find Windows on the hard disk drive in which you are currently located. This can occur for any of these three reasons: (1) Windows might not be installed; (2) Windows may be installed incorrectly; or (3) the Windows directory path name was not added to the system's current search PATH which your computer searches through to locate a command or file. First, check to make sure that Windows is installed. Follow these instructions:

- Type DIR/W \Windows and then press ↵.

If you see the message

File not found

then you did not install Windows or you installed it on a different drive than drive C. Change to any other drive (D, E, and so on) and try again. If you find Windows on another drive, you have to change to that drive and change to the Windows directory before starting Windows.

If a directory listing does appear, look for files that begin with WIN. These are the Windows system files and they must be on your disk to run Windows. If they are not present, perform the installation following the instructions in Appendix A.

MISSING DOS PATH COMMAND

When you perform a custom installation, you are given the option of modifying the AUTOEXEC.BAT file. This can insert the Windows directory into the command Path definition that will enable you to start Windows from any directory, without requiring you to first change to the Windows directory.

If you selected not to modify the files during installation, or if you accidentally deleted AUTOEXEC.BAT, you will be able to start Windows *only* from the Windows directory. You can change to the Windows directory by typing the command **CD\WINDOWS**, and then you can start Windows itself.

To check AUTOEXEC.BAT for the correct path, follow these steps:

1. Type **CD** to change to the root directory.

2. Type **TYPE AUTOEXEC.BAT** and then press ↵.
Look for a line similar to

PATH C:\DOS;C:\WINDOWS;

Note that your PATH command might include additional directories. If the Windows directory is not listed, you may have skipped that step during the installation process. You can add a directory in the PATH command by following these steps:

3. Write down the PATH command, if any, on a piece of paper exactly as it appears on the screen.

4. Type **COPY AUTOEXEC.BAT + CON: AUTOEXEC.BAT**.

5. Carefully type in the entire PATH command that you copied, then type ;**C:\WINDOWS**; at the end of the PATH command and press ↵.
If the file did not contain a PATH command, type **PATH=C:\WINDOWS**;, then press ↵.

6. Type **SET TEMP=C:\WINDOWS\TEMP**, and press ↵.

This tells Windows where to store the temporary files that it creates while it is running. The Windows installation program automatically creates the WINDOWS\TEMP subdirectory.

7. Press Ctrl-Z, and then press ↵.

If Windows is installed and is included in the PATH command but it still will not start, you should perform a reinstallation following the instructions in Appendix A.

Windows Operating Modes

When you start Windows by typing **WIN**, Windows determines the type of computer you are using and selects the appropriate *operating mode*.

If you are using a computer with less than 2MB of memory, Windows starts in the *Standard* mode. In Standard mode, you can run Windows applications in their own windows, and run DOS applications full-screen (but not in their own windows).

If you are using a 386 or 486 computer with at least 2MB of memory, Windows starts in 386 Enhanced mode. In this mode, you'll be able to run both Windows and DOS applications in their own windows.

However, even if you have a 386 or 486 computer with over 2MB of memory, you may find that Windows applications will perform much better in Standard mode. So unless you specifically want to run DOS applications in their own windows (or a Windows application that requires Enhanced mode), start Windows by typing **WIN/S**. This forces Windows to begin in Standard mode.

The Windows Screen

As soon as you start Windows, you can see immediately that it offers an enhanced way of working with your computer. The DOS prompt has been replaced by a graphic interface—images called icons appear on-screen that represent documents, programs, or program groups.

Now that you've started Windows, let's take a look at the parts of the Windows screen.

The Desktop

Windows refers to your monitor's screen as the *desktop*. This term suggests how Windows is used to automate some typical tasks that were formerly performed with tools that were usually placed on the top of a desk, items such as a calendar, calculator, and a clock. Superimposed on the desktop are the windows that hold various tools and applications, similar to the in- and out-baskets that you would use to organize your papers. You will understand this analogy better by examining Figure 1.1 again, which shows the electronic versions of these everyday tools in windows on the screen.

The initial Windows screen, shown with the parts labelled in Figure 3.1, contains two windows on the desktop—the Program Manager window and the Main group window which is contained within the Program Manager window.

Icons

Documents, programs, and groups of programs are represented by small graphic symbols called *icons*. Beneath each icon is its name. The icons in the Main group window are listed in Table 3.1. These are called *program icons* because each icon represents a *program* that you can run.

The picture of an icon graphically illustrates the type of program it represents. The icon for the Print Manager program, for example, is shaped like a printer, while the Clipboard icon looks just like a clipboard.

The icons below the Main group window in Program Manager are called *group icons*. These represent collections of *related* programs or files. No matter how you set up Windows, you will see at least three group icons— StartUp, Accessories, and Games. StartUp contains any programs that you want to run every time you start Windows. Accessories contains the Windows desktop tools. Games contains MineSweeper and Solitaire. You may also see an icon for the Applications group, depending on how you set up

Windows and what other programs are on your disk.

Do not confuse groups with directories—they are not the same. A directory is a DOS convention that arranges groups of files on your hard disk. Directories can be compared to drawers in a filing cabinet. To get a file from your filing cabinet you need to know in which drawer (or directory) it is located. A Windows group, however, is a collection of related programs *grouped* in a logical relationship. Note that programs in one group can be located in *different* disk drives and directories. You'll learn how to work with groups in Lesson 31.

As you work with Windows, you will also see program icons appear on the desktop, below the Program Manager window. These icons represent programs that are still running but whose windows you have temporarily minimized to become program icons while you perform some other task.

FIGURE 3.1:

Windows screen with parts labelled.

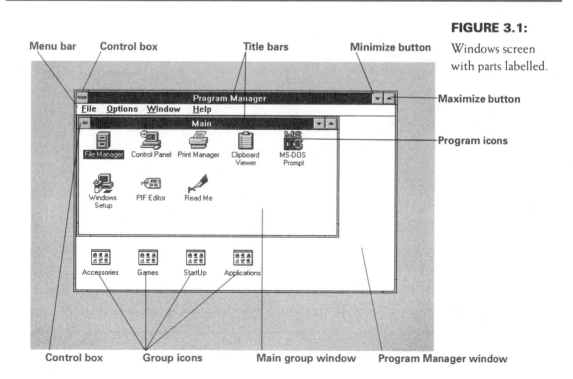

ICON	FUNCTION
File Manager	A program to list, move, copy, and delete files and directories; to change drives and directories; and to format, copy, and erase disks.
Control Panel	A program that provides a graphical way of configuring hardware and changing the Windows environment.
Print Manager	A program for viewing and controlling document printing.
Clipboard Viewer	A program to aid in viewing transferred information between applications or copied information within the same application.
MS-DOS Prompt	A program to return to DOS temporarily.
Windows Setup	A program to modify system settings, set up applications, and add or remove Windows components.
PIF Editor	A program to create or change Program Information Files for DOS applications.
Read Me	Additional information about Windows not found in the User's Guide.

TABLE 3.1:

Icons in the Main Group Window

Title Bar

At the top of each window you will see the *Title bar*, which displays the name of the application being run or the document being used in the window. Notice in Figure 3.1, the Title bars of both the Program Manager and Main windows are highlighted, or appear in reverse video (white on black, or white on blue for color monitors). This indicates that Program Manager is the active application, and Main is the active window running under that application.

There may be times when a window is inactive. Then its Title bar is not highlighted. To run a program or otherwise manipulate a file shown in a window, its window must be active. To select (or activate) a window, click on it anywhere with the mouse and its Title bar will become highlighted.

If you are using a Windows application, the Title bar may also include the name of the file with which you are working, such as the name of the document or drawing.

Menu Bar

In some windows, under the Title bar you will see a *Menu bar*. The Menu bar lists the functions that you can perform. You'll learn how to use the Menu bar in Lesson 4.

In Figure 3.1, the Program Manager window has a Menu bar, the Main group window does not. The Menu bar shows four functions: they are File, Options, Window, and Help. Windows with Menu bars are called *application windows;* they represent a program that you are running. Windows that do not contain Menu bars are called either *document windows* or *group windows*.

A document window contains information that you are using, such as a directory listing in File Manager, or a file that you are creating or editing with an application, such as a word processing program. A group window contains logically related program icons.

A document window is *always* contained in an application window. A group window is always in the Program Manager window. So in this instance, Main is a group window contained within the Program Manager application window, representing a parent-child relationship.

As you work with Windows, you will learn other differences between document and application windows.

Minimize and Maximize Buttons

On the far right of the Title bar there are two buttons with up- and down-pointing arrows.

The down-pointing arrow is called the *minimize button*. Clicking with the mouse on this button reduces the window to an icon and moves it to the bottom of the desktop. The purpose of minimizing a window in this manner is to have it occupy as little room as possible on the screen without actually exiting the application.

The up-pointing arrow is called the *maximize button*. Clicking on this button expands the window so that it will fill the entire screen covering all other windows in the background. Once you maximize a window, the maximize button will then become an up- and down-pointing arrow, and then it is called the *restore button*. Clicking on the restore button restores the window to its previous size.

When you maximize a document window, by clicking on the maximize button in its Title bar, it expands to fill the application window. The document window's title is added to the application window's Title bar, and the document's restore button appears on the application window's Menu bar.

Note that if you do not have a mouse, you can perform these same actions using the keyboard and the Control box. You will learn how to work with the keyboard and the Control box in Lesson 4.

The Control Box

The box on the left of the Title bar is called the *Control box*. Click on the Control box to pull down the Control menu shown in Figure 3.2. The Control menu permits you to perform the following actions: move a window; minimize, maximize, or restore the window; close the document or quit the application; and switch to another application window.

You can display a similar Control menu for group icons and for any temporarily minimized program or document icon. Click on the icon to display the menu. You'll learn more about working with icons in later lessons.

If more than one window is displayed, click on the Control box of the window that you want to manipulate. For example, if you click on the Control box in the application window's Title bar, you can manipulate the application window. If you click on the document window's Control box, you can manipulate the document window.

The Restore, Minimize, and Maximize options in the drop-down Control menu perform the same functions as the restore, minimize and maximize buttons on the right of the Title bar.

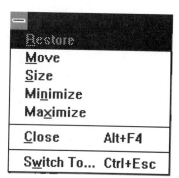

FIGURE 3.2:

The Control menu allows you to manipulate the window or switch to another application.

FEATURING

Drop-down menus
The Control box
Scroll bar
Dialog boxes

▼

Communicating with Windows

ou communicate with Windows with a mouse by pointing to the function that you want to perform and clicking the left mouse button. As stated in Lesson 1, having a mouse is not an absolute necessity with Windows. Every task that you can perform with a mouse can also be performed using the keyboard. In fact, Windows provides a number of shortcut keys for some of the most important functions.

Using the Mouse and the Keyboard

Shortcut keys are keystrokes that you press to perform a function without having to traverse through menus or move your hands from the keyboard. For example, you can quickly arrange multiple windows on the screen by pressing the Shift-F4 combination. This is equivalent to pulling down the Window menu and selecting the Tile option. Since these shortcuts can be quite useful, we'll include the shortcut keys for the functions described in this book.

Even with the shortcut keys, however, a mouse certainly makes Windows easier to use. If you use only the keyboard without a mouse, you lose much of the ease of use for which Windows was designed. In this lesson, you'll learn how to interact with various parts of Windows by using the mouse and the keyboard.

Throughout this book you will be given instructions to highlight and select icons and options. To *highlight* means to place the cursor on the icon or menu option so that its name becomes highlighted or appears in reverse video (white on black). Highlighting does not perform any action immediately; it prepares the icon or option for some action. Often, highlighting is performed with the *keyboard* to prepare an item for selection. For example, you can highlight a Menu bar option with the keyboard without displaying its drop-down menu by pressing the Alt key.

To *select*, however, means to choose an icon or an option in such a way that it performs an action. Selecting a Menu bar option with the mouse, for example, will cause its drop-down menu to display on-screen.

DROP-DOWN MENUS

A *drop-down menu* lists specific operations that you can perform. For example, Figure 4.1 shows the File drop-down menu in the Program Manager window. Notice that the first option, New, is highlighted, or appears in reverse video. This means that the Program Manager is ready to add a file to a group or to create a group. In some drop-down menus, certain options may appear gray or dimmed. This means that these options are not currently available for selection. You must first perform some other function before they can be activated.

Some of the options in a menu show a key or key combination, called shortcut keys, listed to the right of the command. For example, notice the word Del to the right of the menu option Delete in Figure 4.1. This means that you can perform the delete operation by pressing the Del key without having to pull down the menu at all. Sometimes, to use shortcut keys, you must use a key combination, which means press and hold two or more keys at the same time. In Figure 4.1, if you wanted to use the Properties option, you would press and hold the Alt key and the ↵ key together at the same time.

Other options in drop-down menus contain special symbols. An ellipsis (...) following an option name means that if you select that option, a dialog box containing additional choices from which you can make a selection will be displayed. An option name with a triangle symbol (➤) next to it will display another drop-down menu. A check mark (✓) next to a menu option shows that it has been turned on, or that the option is currently selected.

To Display a Drop-Down Menu

- Move the mouse pointer onto the menu name, then click the left mouse button.

or

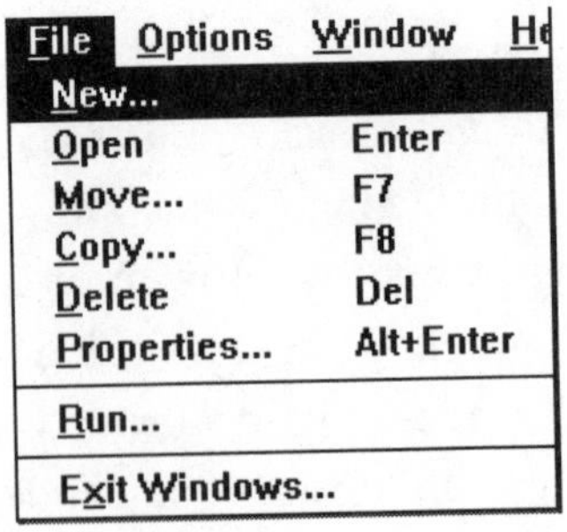

FIGURE 4.1:

The Menu bar shown with the drop-down menu for the File option.

■ Hold down the Alt key and press the *underlined* letter of the menu name, such as Alt-F to display the File menu. Note that the underlined letter is not always the first letter of the word.

To Display Another Drop-Down Menu

■ Click on another menu name in the Menu bar.

or

■ Press the → or ← key to display another menu.

To Select a Drop-Down Menu Option

■ Click on the option with the left mouse button.

or

■ Press the underlined letter.

or

■ Press the ↓ or ↑ key to highlight the menu choice, and then press ↵.

To Cancel a Menu

■ Click anywhere on the outside of the menu screen.

or

■ Press the Esc key.

Working with the Control Box

As mentioned in Lesson 3, the Control box allows you to manipulate the size and position of a window. If you do not have a mouse, you will have to use the Control box quite frequently as you work with Windows.

To Open the Control Box

■ Click on the Control box.

or

■ Press Alt-spacebar to display the Control box menu for *application windows*, such as Program Manager or Paintbrush.

or

■ Press Alt-hyphen to display the Control box menu for *document* or *group windows*. Remember, windows such as Main and Accessories are group windows and considered to be documents of the Program Manager application.

To Close the Control Box Menu

■ Click anywhere on the screen.

or

■ Press the Esc key.

How to Scroll Windows

At times, you'll be working with a window that is too small to display its entire contents. When this occurs, you will see scroll bars along the right side and/or the bottom of the window, as shown in Figure 4.2. You use the scroll bars to bring into view icons, text, or graphics that belong to a window, but are not showing in the window.

The small square inside the scroll bar is called the *scroll box*, or the *elevator*. The position of the scroll box represents that portion of the window you are viewing. For example, when the scroll box is at the bottom of the bar, you are viewing objects at the bottom of the window.

USING THE SCROLL BAR WITH THE MOUSE

Follow these steps to scroll through a window using the scroll bar:

Line-by-line	Click the up- and down-arrow buttons on the ends of a vertical scroll bar to scroll up or down. Use the left and right arrow buttons on a horizontal scroll bar to move the screen left or right.
Screen-by-screen	Click above or below (or to the right or the left of) the scroll box.
To a specific position	Drag (click and hold the left mouse button, then move) the scroll box to the relative position in the scroll bar.

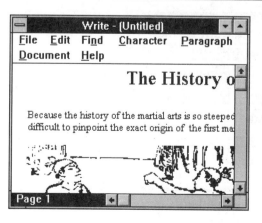

FIGURE 4.2:

The scroll bar appears when the window cannot display all of its information at one time.

SCROLLING WITH THE KEYBOARD

Press the ←, →, ↑, or ↓ keys to scroll through the window line-by-line. The scroll box will move to indicate your position.

In document windows, use the PgUp and PgDn keys to move a screen document several lines at one time.

Working with Dialog Boxes

When you select a menu item or perform an action, you may cause a dialog box to display. Windows displays dialog boxes when it requires you to provide additional information in order to perform a task. A *dialog box* contains options that require some type of user response, which is performed either by clicking on a button or entering some text.

Although some dialog boxes present only a few options, others can be quite complex. The dialog boxes shown in Figure 4.3 and Figure 4.4, for example, contain a number of different types of options.

Here's how you select options in dialog boxes.

MOVING WITHIN A DIALOG BOX

You move from item to item in a dialog box by clicking on the option that you want to choose.

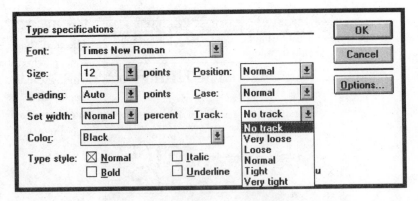

FIGURE 4.3:

Dialog box that contains text boxes, drop-down list boxes, checkboxes, and command buttons. This dialog box is from Aldus Pagemaker.

Using the keyboard, you press Tab to move forward, and Shift-Tab to move backward through the options. You also can press Alt and the underlined letter of the dialog box option in a keystroke combination.

Text Boxes

A *text box* is a boxed area in a dialog box in which you type in information using the keyboard. Figure 4.3, for example, shows three text boxes—Size, Leading and Set width.

You move into a text box by clicking in it with the mouse. If you want to type new information into the box, you must first highlight the existing information. To highlight the text in the text box, place the pointer anywhere in the text and double-click. The highlighted text will be erased when you start typing new information, or when you press Del. To remove the highlighting, click the mouse button anywhere in the box or press any arrow key.

If you move into the textbox using the keyboard, text in the box will become highlighted automatically.

Drop-Down List Boxes

A box that has a down arrow on its right side contains a drop-down list. A *drop-down list* stores options that you can select quickly to insert into a text box. Windows uses these when there are too many options to fit into a dialog box. Figure 4.3 shows eight options with drop-down lists, with the list for the Track option displayed.

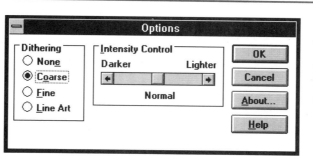

FIGURE 4.4:

This dialog box contains radio buttons and scroll selectors.

To insert an option into the text box from the drop-down list box, first display the box by clicking on the down arrow button at the right of the text box. Then, click on the desired option.

If a drop-down list box is too small to display all of the available options, there will be a scroll bar on the right. Use the scroll bar, as explained earlier in this Lesson, to bring into view additional options that are not shown in the list box:

- Click on the up arrow or down arrow to scroll the list up or down, one item at a time.

- Click above or below the scroll box to scroll the entire list.

- Drag the scroll box to the relative position on the scroll bar where the item you want to select is located.

Note that in some cases, the down arrow is slightly separated from the text box. When the down arrow is separated, you can either select an item from the list box or type your choice directly into the text box. When the arrow is connected to the text box, Windows will not allow you to type in the text box—instead, you must select an option from the list. To cycle through list options with the keyboard, press the ↓ or ↑ key. To display the drop-down list, press Alt-↓.

List Boxes

Some dialog boxes contain list boxes already displayed—you do not have to pull them down. Click on an option in the list box to select it. Double-clicking on an option activates it and then exits the dialog box. Don't double-click until you are finished with the current dialog box options.

Most list boxes are exclusive, that is, you can select only *one* of the listed options—selecting one will remove the highlighting from another. However, there are some list boxes that are nonexclusive, that is, they will allow you to select more than one option. If the options are nonexclusive, click on each one you want to highlight. To deselect a highlighted option, click on it again.

Check Boxes

A *check box* is a small square that you may select. It is located next to an option. When you click on a check box, Windows places an X in the box indicating that the option is turned on. Clicking on a check box that already contains an X removes the X from the check box and turns off the option.

In Figure 4.3, the check boxes determine the format of characters that you can type in Aldus Pagemaker.

In most cases, check boxes are nonexclusive, so you can check more than one box at a time. For example, when entering text, you can select both the bold and underline check boxes to print characters that are both boldfaced and underlined.

With the keyboard, you can toggle a check box on and off by pressing Alt and the underlined letter in the option.

Radio Buttons

A *radio button* is a circle (with a black dot in the center when selected). Grouped radio buttons are mutually exclusive—only one button in a group can be selected at one time. Selecting one button automatically turns off any other button that has been selected.

Figure 4.4 displays a group of radio buttons that control the amount of dithering used to print graphics. (*Dithering* represents colors and shades of gray by various dot sizes.)

You select a radio button by clicking on it or by pressing Alt and the underlined letter in the option.

COMMAND BUTTONS

Selecting a rectangular *command button* will perform an action immediately. Selecting a command button with an ellipsis (...) will display an additional dialog box. Selecting a command button with two > characters (>>) will expand the current dialog box to show additional options.

With a mouse, click on the command button to select it. With the keyboard, if the button has an underlined letter, press Alt and the underlined letter.

Most dialog boxes have command buttons labeled OK and Cancel. Selecting OK accepts the settings in the dialog box and removes it from the screen. Selecting Cancel removes the dialog box but ignores any changes you've made.

To select OK with the keyboard you must press ↵; to select Cancel, you must press the Esc key.

SCROLL SELECTORS

The dialog box in Figure 4.4 contains what looks like a horizontal scroll bar, labelled Intensity Control. The position of the scroll box below the label indicates the setting for this option. In this case, the scroll box is in the center, which represents a normal setting.

To change the setting, click on the ← or →. With the keyboard, highlight the option with the Tab key or by press Alt-I, then press the ← or → to change its setting.

Some scroll selectors may include a text box where you can type in your choice directly. Others will display the setting as you move the scroll box.

FEATURING

**Help drop-down
menus**

**Program
Manager Help
Index**

▼

Getting Help

If you find that you need help when working with Windows, take advantage of the comprehensive Help feature. Help displays screens of information that explain each Windows command and function. By navigating through the Help system, you can pinpoint the specific piece of information that you need.

Almost all Windows applications include a Help option in their Menu bars. Right now, to learn how to use the Help feature select Help from the Menu bar in the Program Manager. Figure 5.1 shows the drop-down menu that is displayed. The options on this menu are described in Table 5.1.

To display a more detailed list of Help topics select a menu option. For example, select Contents to display the screen that is shown in Figure 5.2. (Note that pressing F1 without the Help menu displayed will also bring you to the same screen.)

Notice that some phrases in the figure are underlined. (On a color monitor, these underlined words will also appear in a different color than the other text in the window.) Words or phrases that are underlined are called *hotspots*. When you point to a hotspot, the mouse pointer takes the shape of a small pointing hand.

When you click on a hotspot that is underlined with a *solid line*, Windows will display a screen that contains detailed information about that word or phrase. Other hotspots are underlined with *dotted lines*. When you click on one of these hotspots, a definition of the term will be displayed. When you have finished reading the description, click the mouse button again.

All Help windows contain a Menu bar with the following four options:

File   Select File to open a Help file to be displayed
                        in the Help window; to print the currently
                        displayed Help information, or to exit the Help
                        system.

Help
<u>C</u>ontents
<u>S</u>earch for Help on...
<u>H</u>ow to Use Help
<u>W</u>indows Tutorial
<u>A</u>bout Program Manager...

FIGURE 5.1:

The Help menu displays options for using the Help system.

OPTION	ACTION
Contents	Displays an alphabetical listing of major Help topics.
Search for Help on	Allows you to select help from a list of keywords or enter a subject with which you need help.
How to Use Help	Displays information on using the Help system.
Windows Tutorial	Begins an interactive lesson on using the mouse with Windows.
About Program Manager	Reports the version of Windows, the serial number, the operating mode, and the amount of memory available on your system.

TABLE 5.1:

Help Menu Options

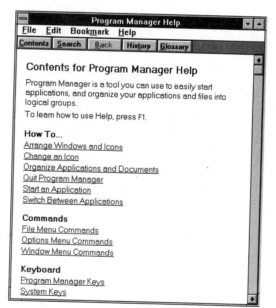

FIGURE 5.2:

Program Manager's Help contents window shows you how to get specific kinds of help.

Edit
: Select Edit to make a copy of the currently displayed Help information that you can then insert into your document, or to annotate your Help file. You'll learn about inserting text in Lesson 29.

Bookmark
: Select Bookmark to mark your place in the Help system. If you use the Bookmark, the Bookmark name will be added to the Bookmark menu. Selecting the Bookmark name returns you to that location quickly when you need help again.

Help
: Select Help to get information about using the Help function and the Help system itself, and to learn how to set the Help window to always be placed at the top of the other windows.

A Button Bar is located just below the Menu bar. This bar contains command buttons that allow you to navigate easily through the Help system, as explained in Table 5.2.

Let's see how to use the Help system to locate some helpful information.

1. Select Help from the Menu bar in the Program Manager to display the Help menu, and then select Contents—point to the word Contents and click the left mouse button.

2. Point to the phrase File Menu Commands and click the left mouse button to display the window shown in Figure 5.3.

Each File menu option is defined and includes underlined hotspots for displaying additional information.

OPTION	ACTION
Contents	Displays the Help index screen.
Search	Allows you to select help from a list of keywords or enter a subject with which you need help.
Back	Displays the Help screen previously displayed. This button will not be active when you first start Help.
History	Displays a list box showing the Help screens you've been using during your current Windows session. The most recent screen will be at the top of the list. You can return to a screen by selecting its name in the list.
Glossary	Presents an alphabetical list of hotspots you can select to display definitions.

TABLE 5.2:

Help Command Buttons

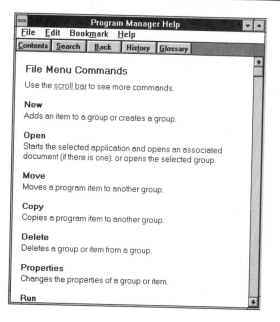

FIGURE 5.3:

The Help window on File Menu Commands shows the functions of different File menu options.

Notice the hotspot for the phrase "scroll bar," which is underlined with a dotted line. To learn more about scroll bars, click on the underlined phrase.

Now, suppose you want to find out how to create a group. Rather than returning to the Contents window, we'll use the Search command button.

3. Select Search to display the dialog box shown in Figure 5.4.

4. Press C.

The list box automatically scrolls to display the first topic that starts with the letter C. However, the topic we are searching for is not shown.

5. Type **R**. The list now scrolls to display the first topic starting with the characters CR.

6. Double-click on the phrase creating groups. The selected option now appears in the bottom list box. Note that when you select some Help topics, several related subjects will appear in the bottom list box.

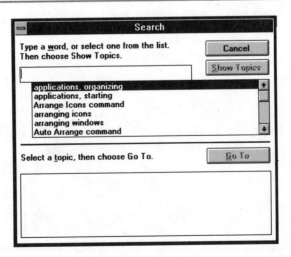

FIGURE 5.4:

The Search dialog box allows you to search for Help topics.

7. Now double-click on the phrase Creating and Deleting Groups in the bottom list box. A Help window will appear with information about this topic.

8. Double-click on the Help window Control box to quit the Help system. (With the keyboard, press Alt-F4.)

In most Windows applications, you would press F1 to get context-sensitive help. Context-sensitive help means information about the menu, dialog box, or function that you are working with when you press F1. If you are not performing a specific function, F1 usually displays the Contents for Program Manager's Help Feature.

FEATURING

**Exiting from
Program
Manager**

**Saving your
Windows setup**

▼

Ending Your
Windows Session

Naturally, when you have finished working with Windows and Windows applications, you will want to exit the Windows program. Make sure to *never* turn off your computer without first formally exiting Windows. If you do, unsaved changes that you have made to documents or other files will not be recorded on the hard disk. Also, you risk permanently damaging your applications and other files.

Saving Your Windows Setup

By default, Windows keeps track of any changes you make to the arrangement of windows on the desktop. So, the next time you start Windows, the screen will appear just as it did when you last exited Windows.

This can be quite useful if you want a different window than Main to appear each time you start Windows. However, often you will open another group window just to run a program during a particular Windows session. If you exit Windows while that group window is displayed, it will reappear with each Windows session.

Let's turn off this feature now so you can work with Windows without having to worry about how the arrangement of the Windows desktop will appear at a later time.

1. Select Options from the Menu bar in Program Manager to display the drop-down menu shown in Figure 6.1. The check mark next to the Save Settings on Exit option indicates that the function is turned on.

2. Select Save Settings on Exit to turn off this feature.

If you later want to save changes you make to the desktop, pull down the Options menu and select Save Settings on Exit again.

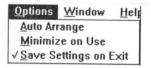

FIGURE 6.1:

Program Manager's Options menu is shown with the Save Settings on Exit option turned on.

Exiting Windows from Program Manager

To exit Windows from the Program Manager window follow these steps:

1. Point to the Program Manager's Control box and double-click, or select Exit Windows from the File drop-down menu. You will see the Exit Windows dialog box (Figure 6.2).

2. Click on OK or press ↵ to exit. To remain in Windows, click on Cancel or press Esc.

Exiting Windows from an Application

If you are running a Windows application, such as Excel or Word for Windows, you must first exit the application before leaving Windows. You can exit the application by double-clicking on its Control box. Using the keyboard, press Alt-F4 or pull down the Control box menu and select Close.

If you try to close an application before saving a changed file, you will see a dialog box similar to Figure 6.3. The dialog box may differ depending on the application. Select Yes to save the changes before exiting, No to exit without saving the changes, or Cancel to remain in the application.

Once the application is closed, you can then exit Windows.

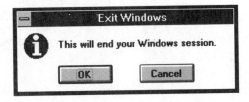

FIGURE 6.2:

Use Exit Windows dialog box to end your Windows session.

EXITING WINDOWS FROM A DOS APPLICATION

If you are running a DOS application from within Windows, you must also exit the application before quitting Windows. Use the program's own commands for quitting to return to the Program Manager, then exit Windows.

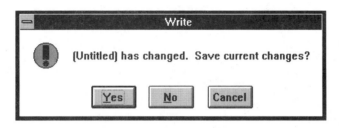

FIGURE 6.3:

A dialog box appears warning that you are attempting to exit an application without saving an edited document.

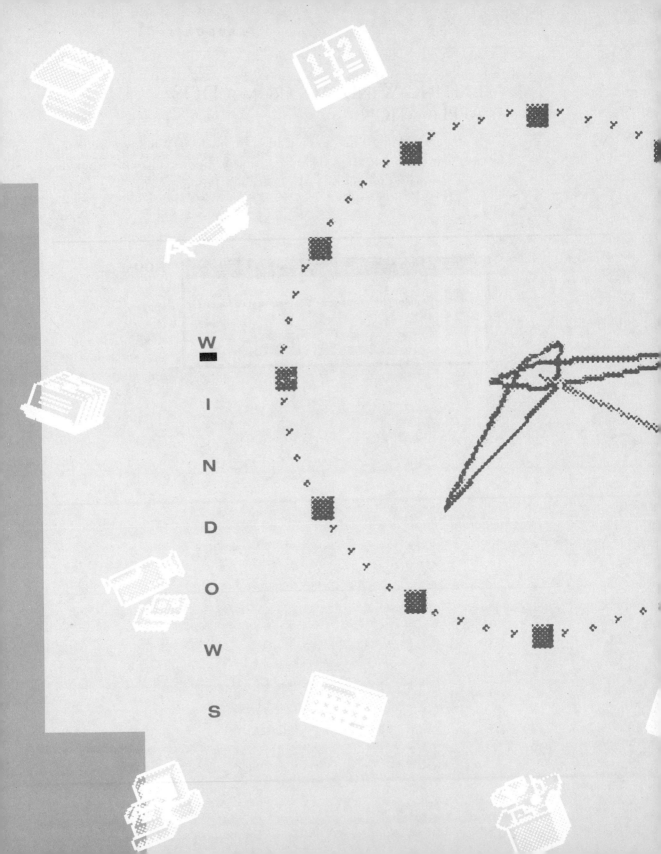

W
I
N
D
O
W
S

PART 2

Working with Windows

Windows takes its name from the windows it uses to display information on your screen. Using these windows, you can work with more than one program at a time and easily transfer information between programs. When you learn to work with individual windows, you are mastering the Windows program itself.

Lesson 7 teaches you how to run and exit Windows applications. Lesson 8 discusses working with multiple applications. Lessons 9 and 10 cover the subjects of maximizing and minimizing windows and icons; moving windows and icons around on the screen; arranging multiple windows and icons; and resizing application and document windows.

Running and Exiting Windows Applications

FEATURING

Running a program from an icon

Closing a window

Opening an application from an iconized group

▼

When you select a program icon from a group window, you run or execute the program. This is one of the easiest ways to run a program, because you can arrange Windows so that the group appears automatically when you start Windows.

In this lesson, you'll learn how to run a program that is in a group, and how to exit the program to return to Program Manager.

To Run a Program from an Icon

In later lessons, you will learn how to add and delete programs from groups. For the time being, however, let's see how you can run a program that's already been assigned to the Main group.

To run a program from an icon you can use any one of these three methods:

- Double-click on the icon.

- Press the ←, →, ↑, or ↓ key until the name under the icon becomes highlighted, then press ↵.

- Highlight the icon, and then select Open from Program Manager's File drop-down menu, or press ↵.

Now, let's try this by running Windows Setup program. If necessary, start Windows.

- Select Windows Setup using any of the methods described above.

The Windows Setup program executes and opens its own window, as shown in Figure 7.1. Notice that it has its own Title bar and Menu bars, which should help you to recognize that it is an application window, not a document window. It has a Control box and a minimize

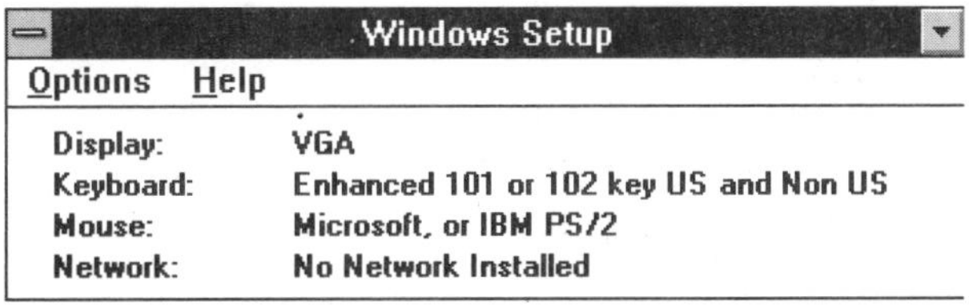

FIGURE 7.1:

The Windows Setup program is executed.

button. It does not have a maximize button, which means that it cannot be run full-screen.

Because the window is active, the Program Manager and Main windows in the background become inactive and their Title bars are no longer highlighted.

Closing a Window

Closing a window means to stop or end the program's execution. When you close any application window except Program Manager, the window is cleared from the screen and Program Manager is displayed. Closing the application does not affect any other program that may be running. For example, you might be writing a document in Write and creating a spreadsheet in Microsoft Excel. Each application would be open in its own window. When you finish editing the document in Write, you would be able to close that window without having to exit Excel.

If you close the Program Manager window, you end the Windows session. Closing a group window in Program Manager, however, reduces it to an icon without ending the Windows' session.

There are several ways to close a window. Using the mouse, the quickest way is to double-click on the window's Control box. You can also use any one of the following procedures:

- Pull down the Control box and select Close.

- Close document windows by pressing Ctrl-F4.

- Close application windows by pressing Alt-F4.

- Select File, and then Exit.

Now close the Windows Setup program to return to the Program Manager.

■ Double-click on the Control box or press Alt-F4.
The window disappears and the Main window becomes active.

Opening an Application from Icon Group

If you want to run a program in the Accessories, Games, or any other group that is a minimized icon in Program Manager, you must first open the group window. When you select a group icon, that opens the group's window and displays its contents. Then you can select the icon to run the program.

TO OPEN A GROUP WINDOW

Follow this procedure to open a minimized group window:

■ Double-click on the icon.

■ Press Ctrl-F6 or Ctrl-Tab to highlight the icon, and then press ↵.

Let's try to open a group window now.

1. First, let's open the Accessories group. Double-click on the Accessories icon, or press Ctrl-Tab until the icon is highlighted, then press ↵.

You now have two group windows open—Main and Accessories. (See Figure 7.2.) The Accessories window is active—observe that its Title bar is in reverse video and it has a Control box and minimize and maximize buttons. The other open group window, Main, is inactive but parts of it can still be seen in the background.

2. Select the Paintbrush program. The Paintbrush program is executed. (See Figure 7.3.)

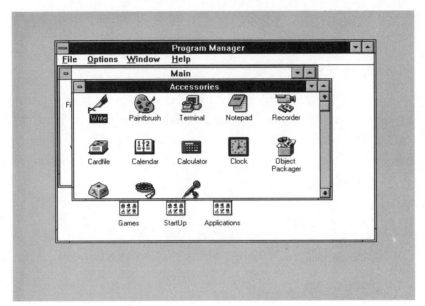

FIGURE 7.2:
The Accessories group window is open.

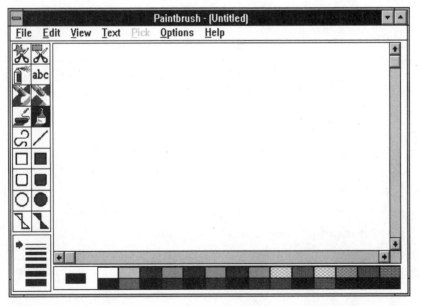

FIGURE 7.3:
The Paintbrush program is executed from the Accessories group.

3. Close Paintbrush. Double-click on the Control box or press Alt-F4.

4. Close the Accessories group window. Double-click on the Control box or press Ctrl-F4.

5. Exit Windows.

OPENING GROUP WINDOWS WITH THE WINDOW MENU

You can also open a group window by using the Window drop-down menu, shown in Figure 7.4. Each of your groups will be listed and numbered at the bottom of the menu. To open a group, select its name or press the number next to its name.

Note that because Windows provides multitasking, you do not have to exit an application program in order to return to Program Manager. In the next lesson you'll learn how to work with more than one application and window.

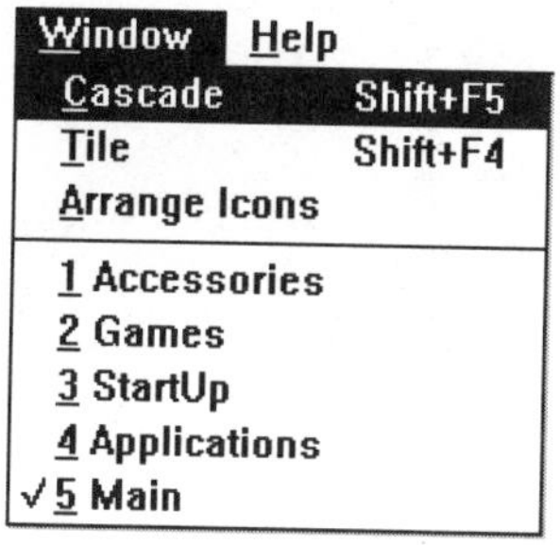

Window	Help
Cascade	Shift+F5
Tile	Shift+F4
Arrange Icons	
1 Accessories	
2 Games	
3 StartUp	
4 Applications	
√ 5 Main	

FIGURE 7.4:

The Window drop-down menu will allow you to open a group window.

Working with Multiple Windows Applications

Your desk probably contains papers, reports, folders, and books that relate to a number of different projects. Instead of completely cleaning off your desk when you change projects, most likely you just move one set of papers out of the way to make room for new ones. In this manner, you can switch back and forth between projects easily and you are still able to refer to any paper or folder on your desk when you need it.

The Windows desktop works the same way. You can run several programs and accessories simultaneously, each in its own window. Each window represents an active program and you can switch between them quickly, or refer to the clock, calendar, or any other accessory when needed. Note that when you switch out of an application you are not closing it; switching simply moves the application to the background on the desktop.

There are a variety of techniques for working with multiple applications. In this lesson, you will learn the fundamental procedures for opening several applications and switching between them.

In the following steps you'll learn how to work with multiple windows by opening several of the programs in the Accessories group. These applications are discussed in greater detail in Part Four of this book. For this lesson, just follow these steps:

1. Start Windows.

2. Open the Accessories group using one of the procedures described in Lesson 7.

3. Now, select the Main window again. Click anywhere on the Main window that you can see behind the Accessories window.

4. Select the Accessories window again.

5. Select the Clock accessory. Point to the Clock icon and double-click the left mouse button. The Clock window opens in the foreground. (See Figure 8.1.)

6. Select the Accessories window again.

7. Select Calendar to display the calendar application.

8. Select the Accessories window again. Note that this may be difficult if you are using the mouse because most of the

Accessories window may be covered by other windows. Position the mouse pointer carefully on any part of the window that is still showing.

If you cannot click on a window because it is totally hidden in the background, you can use the Task List which is explained later in this lesson. You can also switch windows using the shortcut keys listed in Table 8.1. These shortcut keys are particularly useful if you have a large number of application and document windows open simultaneously.

9. Select Calculator.

At this point you are running three accessory applications at the same time.

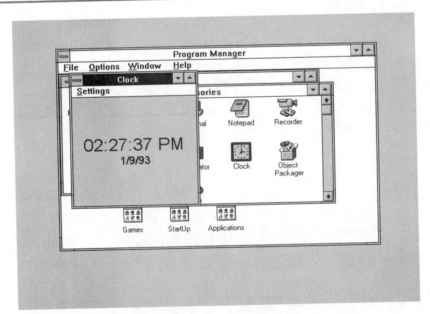

FIGURE 8.1:

The Clock window is displayed in the foreground over other open windows.

SHORTCUT KEY	FUNCTION
Ctrl-Tab	Cycles between group icons and open group windows.
Alt-Tab	Press Alt-Tab to switch to the last used application. Hold down the Alt key and press Tab to see the titles of all open applications. Release the Alt key when the title appears in the foreground for the application you want.
Alt-Esc	Cycles through *all* running applications. It will highlight an icon on the desktop, but it will not open it.

TABLE 8.1:

Shortcut Keys for Changing Windows

Using the Task List

If you cannot click on a window because it is entirely in the background, you can switch windows using the Task List. The Task List is a dialog box that lists the names of all applications that are currently running. (See Figure 8.2.)

Display the Task List by pulling down the Control menu of the application window in the foreground and selecting Switch To or double-click on the blank area of the screen. The shortcut keystroke for displaying the Task List is Ctrl-Esc.

To select a window from the Task List, double-click on its name, or highlight the name and select Switch To.

To close a window from the Task List, highlight its name and select End Task.

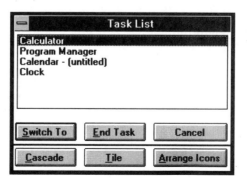

FIGURE 8.2:

The Task List can be used to switch applications.

We'll discuss the other Task List options in Lesson 10.

Note that the Control menus of group and document windows do not contain the Switch To option. Instead, they have the Next (Ctrl-F6) option. Use Next to cycle through document windows. If you are in Program Manager, Next cycles through open group windows and group icons.

Closing Multiple Windows

When you are ready to quit Windows you should exit each of the open applications. You can double-click on their Control boxes, press Alt-F4, select Close from the Control menu, or Exit from the File drop-down menu. You will be warned if you make any changes to the open documents.

You can exit Windows quickly by switching to, and then closing the Program Manager window. Do this now.

1. Click the Control box and select Switch To to display the Task List.

2. Highlight Program Manager.

3. Click on End Task.

You will see the Exit Dialog box, as discussed in Lesson 6. If you select OK but you haven't saved a document in an open application, Windows will display the warning dialog box asking you whether you want to save the file. To save the file, select Yes—Windows will return to the application and display its Save dialog box. Save the file, and then exit Windows.

Windows will not allow you to exit if you still have a DOS application open in the background. It will display a warning dialog box with the name of the open application displayed in the Title bar. Select OK, close the application, and then exit Windows.

Minimizing and Maximizing Windows

Having your desktop full of background windows can be fairly distracting. Rather than working with a cluttered screen, you can choose either to maximize the application you are working with so that it fills the entire desktop, or to minimize the windows you are not working with so that they appear reduced as icons. In this lesson you will learn how to use both methods.

Maximizing an Open Window

Usually, when you open an application, its window will not fill the entire screen but will appear instead as a window overlapping those windows that are already displayed. However, if you are working with a word processing program or some other major application, you will want to see as much of your work full-screen as is possible. The difficulties of writing a report are certainly intensified if you can view only half of each line.

You can display your work full-screen by maximizing the application's window after you have opened it. When you *maximize* a window, it is enlarged so that it fills the entire screen or desktop. Any other open windows are then moved into the background.

To maximize a window, you can click on the maximize button, or you can select the Control box first and then select Maximize from the Control menu.

The window will fill the entire screen and the maximize button will change into a restore button with up- and down-pointing arrows. To return the window to its previous size, click on the restore button, or select the Control box and then select Restore.

Reducing Applications to Icons

The other way to remove clutter from your desktop is to minimize the application windows that you are not using. Minimizing a window reduces it to an icon without closing the application. If you later enlarge the application and change it back to a window, your work will be in place and unchanged, unless it is performing some task in the background, such as running or compiling a program.

A minimized application window icon is not the same as the application program icon in a group window. The icon that represents the minimized window appears at the bottom of the desktop, not in the Program Manager window, and it represents a program that is already loaded into your computer's memory. The icon in the group window represents the program's executable file on the disk. You'll see the important differences between these icons shortly.

Note that if you are running Program Manager or some other window full-screen, you will not be able to see the icons that represent minimized applications unless you restore or minimize the full-screen application's window.

When you want to work with the minimized application, you can restore or maximize its window.

Now, to see how this works let's use the Calendar window.

1. Start Windows.

2. Double-click on the Accessories group icon.

3. Double-click on the Calendar icon in the Accessories group to run the Calendar application.

4. Minimize the window—click on the minimize button.

The window becomes an icon and moves to the bottom of the desktop. (See Figure 9.1.) Beneath the icon is the name of the application

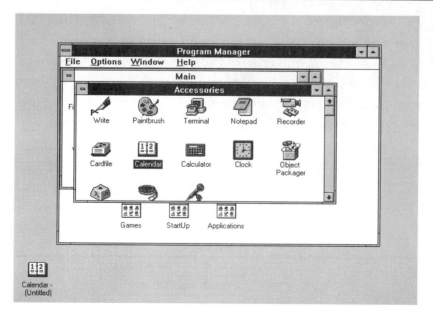

FIGURE 9.1:

The Calendar window is minimized to an icon.

with the word *[untitled]* under the name. This means that the current document in the application—the calendar that is being created—has not yet been named. (You'll learn how to create and use calendars in Lesson 25.)

Expanding an Icon to a Window

When you want to continue working with the minimized application, you expand its icon which is located on the bottom of the desktop. Expanding an icon returns the application to a window.

You can expand an icon into a window in several ways. *Restoring* the icon changes the window to the size it was before you minimized it. Maximizing the icon cause the window to display full-screen.

If the icon is not hidden behind a full-screen window, and appears on the desktop, you can enlarge it easily by double-clicking on the icon to restore it to its previous size.

If you click once on the icon, its Control menu will appear, as shown in Figure 9.2. Select Restore or Maximize to open the window.

Often, your desktop will be arranged so that you will see both the minimized program icon on the desktop, and the application's icon in the group window in Program Manager. To expand the program, you must use the icon on the desktop which represents the running application. If you select the icon in Program Manager, you actually will start a second copy of the same application. Then, you will have two versions of the same program running—one on-screen in a window and another still minimized as an icon. Note that any work you started

FIGURE 9.2:

The Control menu of an icon is shown on the desktop.

in the minimized version will not appear in the second copy of the program.

Clicking once on a group icon in Program Manager displays the group's Control menu as well. You can then open the group window by selecting Restore or Maximize.

Minimizing Program Manager Automatically

You can minimize Program Manager just as you can any other window. Minimizing Progam Manager will leave a clear desktop so that only your current running applications will be displayed. (See Figure 9.3.)

You can also minimize Program Manager automatically when you start any program. This will save you the trouble of switching to Program Manager and minimizing it after you've started the other program. To minimize Program Manager automatically, select Options from the Menu bar, and then select Minimize on Use.

If you also select Save Settings on Exit (with a check mark showing next to it), this option will be recorded on your hard disk and used when you next start Windows. This means that the settings in your current desktop will be retained when you next start Windows.

FIGURE 9.3:

Clear desktop is shown with minimized Program Manager.

Changing the Size and Position of Windows and Icons

In addition to restoring, minimizing, and maximizing windows, you can move their position on the screen, and you can resize most windows in small increments. Remember, in order to resize or move a window, the window must be open and not maximized.

Changing the Size of a Window

You can change the size of any window that has borders made of double lines. This includes Program Manager, group windows, and most application windows. Most warning and confirmation dialog boxes, however, *cannot* be resized. They have single-line borders and require an immediate response from you. Note that the Calculator window, which also has single-line borders, can be restored, maximized, and minimized, but it cannot be resized.

To change the size of a window, follow these steps:

1. Point to one of the window's borders or corners. The mouse pointer will change to a double-pointed arrow.

   ■ Point to the top or bottom border to change the window's height.

   ■ Point to the right or left border to change the window's width.

   ■ Point to one of the corners to change both the height and width at the same time.

2. Click and hold the left mouse button.

3. Drag the mouse out and away from the window to enlarge the window, or inward to reduce it.

As you drag the mouse, an outline of the corresponding border or corner will move along with it. (See Figure 10.1.)

4. Drag the mouse until the window is the desired size, and then release the mouse button.

Obviously, you cannot make an application window any larger than the desktop, which is limited by the size of your screen. Similarly, you can maximize a document window only as large as the space in its application window will allow.

Moving Windows

You cannot move a document window out of an application window. However, you can move it so that it is partially out of view in the application window's work space. If you later have difficulty resizing or moving the document window, maximize the application window. (If you minimize a document window, it reduces to an icon.)

Note that you cannot move most confirmation and warning dialog boxes.

To move a window on the desktop, drag its Title bar. Click anywhere in the Title bar and hold down the left mouse button. As you drag the pointer, an outline of the window will move along with it. Position the outline where you want the window to appear and then release the mouse button.

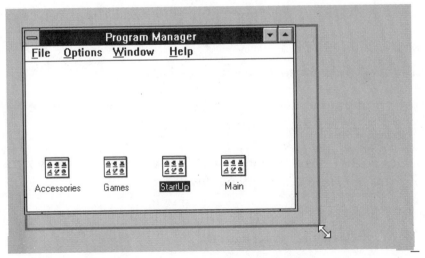

FIGURE 10.1:

As you drag the mouse, an outline of the selected border indicates the new size of the window.

Arranging Windows Using Tile and Cascade

When you have several windows open, the screen can appear to be cluttered. If you need all of the open windows to appear on the screen, however, you can arrange them neatly using either the Tile or Cascade options.

Tiling causes each window to be the same size and displays them side-by-side. Cascading also makes all the windows into the same size, but it causes them to overlap one another neatly.

To tile group windows within the Program Manager window, select Tile from the Window menu, or press Shift-F4. You can cascade windows in Program Manager by selecting Cascade from the Window menu, or by pressing Shift-F5. The Tile and Cascade options do not affect other application windows.

To arrange open application windows on the desktop, including Program Manager, open the Task List by pressing Ctrl-Esc, double-clicking on the blank part of the screen, or selecting Switch To from any application window's Control menu. Then select either Tile or Cascade. Note that the Task List options will not affect open group windows in Program Manager.

Try this now:

1. Start Windows.

2. Open the Clock, Notepad, and Calendar accessories.

3. Open the Task List. Press Ctrl-Esc, double-click on the blank area of the screen, or select Switch To from the Control menu of any application window.

4. Select Tile.

The windows will appear as shown in Figure 10.2. If you selected Minimize on Use, Program Manager would appear as an icon on the bottom of the desktop.

5. Open the Task List.

6. Select Cascade. Figure 10.3 shows the cascaded windows.

7. Exit Windows.

Arranging Icons on the Desktop

You can reposition icons, either on the desktop or in Program Manager by dragging them with the mouse. Click on the icon and hold the left mouse button, then drag the icon to the desired position.

Be sure to keep the following points in mind:

- You cannot move a group icon out of the Program Manager window.

- You cannot move an icon from a group window into the Program Manager window.

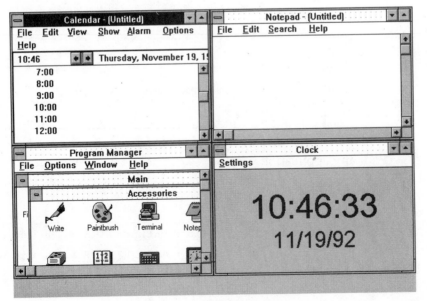

FIGURE 10.2:

Tiled application windows are shown on the desktop.

■ You cannot move an icon representing a minimized window into a window. If you did, it would appear as if the icon were on the window but it would merely be overlapped on top of it.

■ If you have two group windows open, you can move an icon from one to the other. This actually moves the program out of its original group, and inserts it into the new group. You'll learn more about groups and their icons in Lesson 31.

HAVING WINDOWS ARRANGE YOUR ICONS

If you don't like the new position of your icons, you can have Windows neatly arrange them for you. Select Arrange Icons from the Window menu to arrange the position of group icons in the Program Manager window and the individual icons in the active group window. This menu choice does not affect icons of minimized windows on the desktop.

To arrange minimized icons on the desktop, display the Task List and select Arrange Icons.

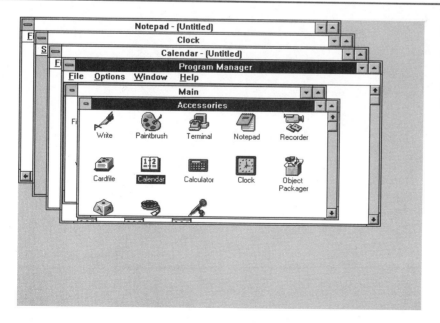

FIGURE 10.3:

Application windows are arranged with the Cascade option.

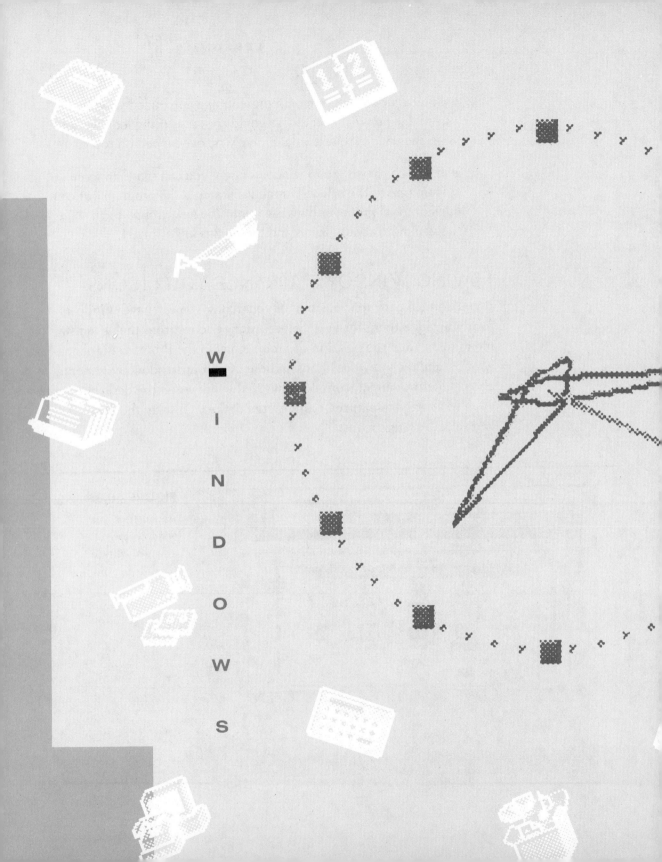

W
I
N
D
O
W
S

PART 3

The File Manager

When you use File Manager it is like having a personal assistant for organizing your files, documents, and directories. Windows' graphic interface, File Manager, helps you to visualize the arrangement and contents of hard disks and floppy diskettes.

Once you've mastered File Manager, you will no longer have to waste precious time searching for files and struggling with commands. You will be able to access even the most complex directory structure quickly and easily.

Getting to Know File Manager

ile Manager is the name of the Windows program that allows you to manipulate files, directories, and disks. It is an important part of Windows that you probably will use frequently. You can use File Manager to perform most of the tasks that you would from the DOS prompt, such as the following:

- Listing directories

- Copying, deleting, and renaming files

- Copying, deleting, and renaming directories

- Creating and changing directories

- Running programs

- Printing text files

- Changing disk drives

- Copying, erasing, and formatting disks

In this lesson, you will start File Manager, adjust its appearance, and change disk drives. In the lessons that follow you will learn how to use File Manager in greater depth.

File Manager Window

Now, let's start File Manager, which by default is the first icon in the Main group window.

1. If necessary, start Windows to display the Main group window. If you are already in Windows and the Main group is not displayed, close your application in order to display the Main group. If Main appears as a group icon in Program Manager, double-click on the icon to restore the window.

2. Start File Manager by double-clicking on its icon in the Main group window, or highlight the icon and press ↵.

Windows scans your hard disk looking for subdirectories and then displays the File Manager window which includes a Title bar and a Menu bar. (See Figure 11.1.) The Menu bar options are described in Table 11.1.

Within File Manager's application window there is a directory document window. On top of this window there is a disk drive icon bar containing icons that represent your disk drives, including any RAM disks and network drives that may be present. The letter designation of each drive (a, b, c, d, and so on) and the current disk drive volume label (if it has one), are displayed to the right of the disk drive icon bar. (The volume label is an optional name that you can assign to a disk when you format it, or when you use the Label command.)

The main section of the directory document window is divided into two parts. On the left there is the directory tree, which is a graphical representation of the relationship between directories and subdirectories. The default directory tree displays directories branching from the root. (Your own directory tree will differ from the one shown in the figure.) In Figure 11.1, the Windows directory is selected, as evidenced by the fact that it is highlighted. When you first start File Manager, the Windows directory is selected by default as indicated by the icon of an open file folder.

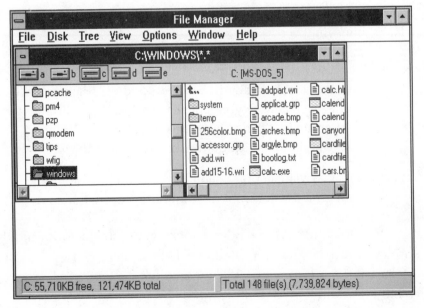

FIGURE 11.1:

File Manager's window includes a Title bar and a Menu bar.

OPTION	OPERATIONS
File	Copy, open, move, rename, delete, and set file properties; run programs; print and associate files with applications; create directories, and search files
Disk	Copy, label, format disks, and make bootable disks; select disk drive
Tree	Expand and collapse directory trees; indicate Expandable Branches
View	Control the contents and order of listed files and directories
Options	Set operation confirmations; change font; save settings on exit; display status bar; minimize directory windows when program is executed
Window	New window, tile, cascade, arrange icons, refresh; select directory windows
Help	Display File Manager Help contents, search for Help on topics; File Manager Help usage; File Manager information

TABLE 11.1:

File Manager Menu Bar Options

The section to the right of the tree displays the names of subdirectories and files contained in the selected directory. In Figure 11.1, the only subdirectories shown are those contained in the Windows directory. As you select directories from the tree on the left, the directory contents listing on the right will change automatically to show the corresponding directory contents.

At the bottom of the File Manager window is the status bar. On the left of the status bar there is information about the current disk drive—its drive letter, the amount of free disk space, and its total capacity. On the right side of the status bar there is information on the current directory—the number of files it contains and the number of bytes they use.

Before continuing with File Manager, let's make sure that you understand the need for directories and subdirectories, and why the analogy of a tree is so appropriate.

Disk Organization

One way to grasp the idea behind directories and subdirectories is to compare your disk drive to a library. If the librarian simply stored all of the books in some random order, it would be close to impossible to locate a particular volume. To make things manageable, the library is divided into sections—fiction, nonfiction, reference, and so forth. Each section is subdivided even further—the nonfiction section, for example, contains subsections for bibliography, science, history, business, and other subjects.

You can locate a book easily by first going to the major section in which it would be located, such as fiction or nonfiction, and then continuing to search each subdivision until you locate the specific book that you want to find.

Your disk drive can be organized just like a library. The root directory can be compared to a library's main lobby. Where a lobby contains information about the divisions within the library and the card catalog, the root directory contains important batch and system files and the directories that stem from the root. In turn, each directory contains its own files and programs, as well as subdirectories. Also, if necessary, the subdirectories can contain their own subdirectories.

The tree diagram is a graphical representation of the relationship between the root, directories, and subdirectories. It shows which directories branch directly from the root, and which subdirectories branch from the directories. For example, Figure 11.2 illustrates a disk drive with three main branches, or directories in the root, namely, EXCEL, WINDOWS and WINWORD. EXCEL is used for spreadsheets, WINDOWS for the Windows system, and WINWORD for word processing.

These subdirectories contain additional branches. DOC, for instance, is a subdirectory within the WINWORD directory. It is not connected to the EXCEL or WINDOWS directory.

Although it is convenient to use the term *branch* when describing disk drives, the term does not fully reflect the relationship between a directory and a subdirectory. Subdirectories do not just branch off from a directory; they are contained within it. For example, the subdirectory

DOC, including any files or subdirectories that it might contain, is *part* of the WINWORD directory. The only way to access files in the DOC directory is to move from the root directory, to the WINWORD directory, and then to the DOC subdirectory.

The terms directory and subdirectory can lead to some confusion. A subdirectory is merely a directory that is contained within another directory. So, technically, even directories that branch directly from the root could be called subdirectories. For ease of nomenclature, however, branches from the root are usually called directories while directories branching from these are called subdirectories.

Because subdirectories are independent of each other, you can have two subdirectories that have the same name, as long as they are not in the same branch level of the tree. If you like, you could have a subdirectory called DOC in the EXCEL directory and one in the WINDOWS directory. You can also have files of the same name so long as

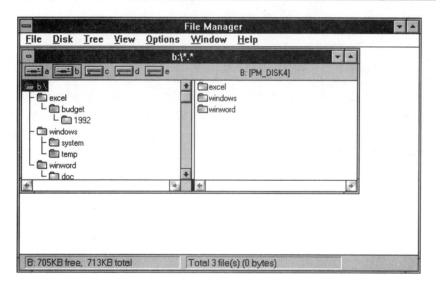

FIGURE 11.2:

Directory tree shown with three directories and various subdirectories.

they are located in different directories. You can name a file BUDGET in DOC and it will not interfere with the file called BUDGET in EXCEL.

How to Change Disk Drives

If you want to access a directory or a file on another disk drive, you first have to activate that drive. You activate a drive by clicking on its icon. The directory tree for that drive will appear in the window.

How to Change the Appearance of File Manager

You can minimize, maximize, resize, or move the File Manager window just as you can any other window. If you want to view as many of the files contained in the directory as possible, then maximize the File Manager window and the directory document as well.

Now, let's look at four other ways to change the amount of information that is displayed in the window.

CHANGING THE VIEW

The split window arrangement can be very convenient when you want to display both the directory tree and the directory contents list at the same time. But when you want to work with just the tree or the directory, it can be distracting.

Using the View menu, you can change File Manager so that it displays only the tree or the directory. This apportions as much window space as is possible to that part of File Manager in which you are interested.

To change the view, select Tree Only or Directory Only from the View menu. (See Figure 11.3.) To return to the default setting, select Tree and Directory. You will learn how to use the other options of the View menu later in Lesson 13.

USING THE SPLIT BAR

The split bar is the very narrow, vertical, white bar between the directory tree area on the left and the directory contents list area on the right. It is just to the right of the vertical scroll bar. If you are viewing *just* the directory tree or *just* the directory contents list, the split bar can be seen on the *left* edge of the window. By moving the split bar, you can change the proportion of the space given to either the directory tree or the directory contents list. Note that if your directory names are short, and you do not have many levels of subdirectories, much of the area devoted to the directory tree will be blank. (Refer again to Figure 11.1.) You can use this space to display file names by moving the split bar to the left, as shown in Figure 11.4.

To move the split bar, point to it. The pointer will change to a black double-pointed arrow with a vertical bar. Press and hold down the left mouse button, drag the bar to the right to reduce the directory contents list area, or to the left to enlarge it, then release the mouse button.

REMOVING THE STATUS BAR

Although the status bar displays some useful information, you can turn it off if you want to devote as much space as possible to the tree or to

View Options Wind
√ Tree and Directory
Tree Only
Directory Only
Split
√ Name
All File Details
Partial Details...
√ Sort by Name
Sort by Type
Sort by Size
Sort by Date
By File Type...

FIGURE 11.3:

The View menu allows you to change the view.

the directory contents list. To toggle the status bar off and on, select Status Bar from the Options menu. The Options menu is shown in Figure 11.5.

CHANGING THE FONT IN FILE MANAGER

A screen font is the type style and size used to display characters on the screen. Windows is supplied with a number of different screen fonts. By default, File Manager uses the font named MS Sans Serif in the 8-point size to display the directory names in the tree, the file names in the directory contents list, and the disk drive letters above the tree. (It is helpful to know that there are approximately 72 points to an inch.)

If you have difficulty reading the screen, you can change the characters to a larger point size or to an entirely different font. You can also reduce the point size to display more information in each window, although the text may become more difficult to read.

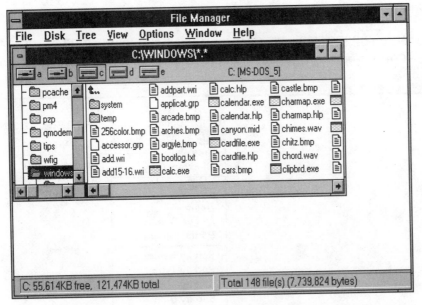

FIGURE 11.4:

Directory window with the split bar moved to display additional files.

To change the font used for File Manager, follow these steps:

1. Select Font from the Options menu. Windows will display the Font dialog box shown in Figure 11.6.

2. Select the font, style, and size you want from the list boxes.

   A sample of what the text looks like will appear in the Sample Box. Select Lower Case to toggle the File Manager to display file and directory names in lower case.

3. Select OK to accept the new font definitions and return to File Manager, or Cancel to discard the changes.

   By the way, the two T's next to Times New Roman and some other fonts indicate True Type fonts. You'll learn about True Type in Appendix B.

Exiting File Manager

When you exit File Manager, by default it automatically saves any changes that you made to the size and position of the window, and any settings that you made with the View and Options menus.

Because we'll be practicing quite a bit with File Manager during the next lessons, let's turn off this feature before exiting File Manager since we will not want to save changes automatically.

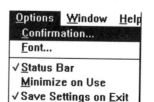

FIGURE 11.5:

The status bar choice in the Options menu toggles on and off the status bar.

1. Select Save Settings on Exit from the Options menu. This turns this feature off, removing the check mark next to the option.

2. Exit File Manager. Double-click on its Control box or press Alt-F4.

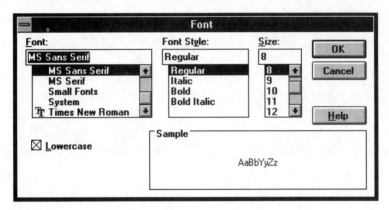

FIGURE 11.6:

The Font dialog box in File Manager allows you to change the screen font, style, and size used by File Manager.

Working with Directory Trees

By default, the directory tree in File Manager displays only the *first level* of directories branching from the root, but not all of the subdirectories. Windows displays this first level of directories to provide an overview of your disk organization. However, this view may not be sufficient. In order to get to a specific file, you must first access its correct drive, as you learned how to do in Lesson 11, and then the next step is to select the directory or subdirectory in which the file is located.

In this lesson, you will learn how to work with the directory tree portion of the File Manager window to display various levels of directories and subdirectories. In Lesson 13, you will learn how to work with the display of the directory contents list.

You work with the directory tree using the mouse, or the Tree menu shown in Figure 12.1. Note that most of the commands in the menu have an associated shortcut key. Remember that a shortcut key is a key or key combination that you can select as a *shortcut* for selecting menu choices. You can activate a menu option with a shortcut key when the menu is not displayed on the screen. For example, you can press Alt-F4 and exit Program Manager at any time.

Selecting a Directory

When you select a directory, its name becomes highlighted, its folder icon appears open, and its contents appear on the right side of the window. Note that if you have a large disk drive with many files, it may take some time for the directory contents list to appear.

To select a directory, click on its folder icon or name. If necessary, you can use the scroll bar to bring the correct portion of the tree into view. Remember, click on the up and down arrows on the ends of the scroll bar to scroll the directory list in small increments. Click above or below the elevator (the small box inside the scroll bar) to scroll one window at a time.

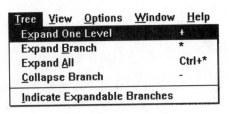

FIGURE 12.1:

Use the Tree menu with shortcut keys to expand or collapse the directory tree.

Indicating Subdirectories

You can tell if the current directory contains subdirectories by looking at the directory contents—subdirectories are indicated by icons that look like folders. This does not, however, inform you about which other directories have subdirectories. To see which directories contain subdirectories, select Indicate Expandable Branches from the Tree menu. File Manager will insert a plus sign (+) on the folders of all the directories that contain subdirectories.

Expanding a Directory

To get a better picture of the directory tree, you can instruct File Manager to expand its display. In the directory tree, expanding will display the names of subdirectories that are contained within the directory.

The root directory is expanded, or displayed with all of its sub-directories, when you start File Manager. If the Indicate Expandable Branches option is on, you'll see a minus sign (−) appear on the root directory's folder. File Manager uses the minus sign to indicate that a branch has been expanded and that its subdirectories are listed on the tree.

To expand a directory, double-click on the directory's folder icon or name, or highlight the directory, then select Expand One Level from the Tree menu (or press +).

Expanding a directory using these methods will display only one additional level of subdirectories. If the Indicate Expandable Branches option is on, a plus sign (+) will appear on the folder of any subdirectory that contains its own subdirectories. This indicates that there are still unexpanded directories in the tree.

To Fully Expand a Selected Directory

To expand a directory so that all levels of its subdirectories will appear on the directory tree, highlight the directory and then select Expand Branch from the Tree menu. Figure 12.2 shows a directory fully expanded.

Note that fully expanding a directory is faster than expanding each of its branches individually.

To Expand the Entire Directory

To expand the entire directory tree, select Expand All from the Tree menu or press Ctrl-*. It does not matter which directory is highlighted.

Collapsing an Expanded Directory

When you don't need to see the subdirectories in a directory, you can *collapse* the directory by using the Tree menu's Collapse Branch option, which removes the branches from view.

To collapse an expanded directory, double-click on the directory's folder icon or name, or highlight the directory and then select Collapse Branch from the Tree menu (or press –). All of the subdirectories below that

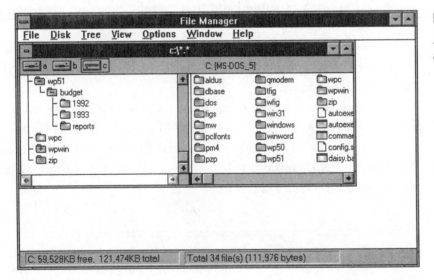

FIGURE 12.2:

A branch fully expanded.

point in the branch will disappear and the minus signs in the directory folders will change to plus signs.

Now, let's practice expanding directories using the methods discussed above.

1. If necessary, start Windows and open File Manager.

2. Collapse the Windows directory if it is expanded—double-click on the Windows folder icon or name, or highlight the Windows folder, then press –.

3. In the same manner, collapse the entire directory tree by double-clicking on the root directory icon.

4. Now expand the root directory one level. Double-click on the root directory icon.

5. Finally, expand the Windows directory. Double-click on its icon to expand the Windows directory.

Refreshing Directory Trees

If you are using Windows 3.1 in a network environment, expanding or collapsing directory trees may not list all of the actual directory names, because another user may have modified the directory since you last used the system.

To display an up-to-date directory tree, press F5 or select Refresh from the Window menu. This will force Windows to rescan the disk for subdirectories.

Working with Directory Listings

If you want to copy, delete, rename, move, and/or print one or more related files, you should first locate the files by using the directory tree and the directory contents list. You do this by finding the directory or subdirectory in which the specific files you want are stored. As you learned in Lesson 11, when you select a directory from the tree, its contents appear on the right side of the window.

In this lesson you will learn the fundamentals of working with the directory contents list. The contents list displays the names of all subdirectories and files in the selected directory. Next to each directory, subdirectory, and file name you will see an icon representing the type of file it is. The meaning of these icons is explained in Table 13.1.

How to Select a File

When you select a file, its name and icon in the directory listing will be highlighted. Selecting the file also activates the directory contents listing portion of the screen. When the directory contents list is active, the highlight in the tree is replaced by a selection box.

To select a file, click either on its name or on its icon.

You will learn how to select multiple files in Lesson 17.

Navigating the Tree from the Directory Contents List

You can move easily between the directory contents list and the tree by clicking the corresponding portions of the screen. File Manager also allows you to change directories from within the directory contents list. This can be useful if you've selected to show only the directory contents list and not the tree.

HOW TO MOVE UP THE BRANCH

At the beginning of each directory contents list you will see the UP icon, an up-pointing arrow followed by two dots. Selecting this icon takes you up one level in the directory tree structure. For example, when the contents of the Windows directory are listed, the UP icon brings you to the root directory. When the System subdirectory is listed, double-clicking on the UP icon brings you to the Windows directory.

To display the contents of the parent (one level up) directory in the tree, double-click on the UP icon. If the tree is displayed on the left, a selection box will surround the directory's name.

ICON	FILE TYPE
🔼..	Up Icon—represents the previous level of the current branch
📁	Subdirectory in the current directory
🗔	Executable program file with EXE, COM, BAT, and PIF extensions
📄	Document file
📄	All other files

TABLE 13.1:

Windows Directory File Icons

To change to an entirely different directory in the tree, double-click on the desired directory.

HOW TO OPEN A SUBDIRECTORY

The names of any subdirectories contained in the directory can be found below the UP icon in the directory contents list.

To change to subdirectories through the directory contents list, double-click on the subdirectory's name or icon.

HOW TO REFRESH THE DIRECTORY CONTENTS LIST

If you are viewing a network drive, the directory contents list will not change automatically if another user changes the directory. To update the directory contents list, press F5 or select Refresh from the Window menu.

You can also use Refresh to see the contents of a different diskette in a floppy drive. The contents of the new diskette will appear in the window.

Displaying Multiple Directories

There may be times when you will find it convenient to display on the screen more than one directory at a time. It is easier to move and copy files when you can simultaneously see both the directory containing the files and the directory you are moving them to. For example, you might want to copy a file from your word processing subdirectory into another subdirectory. To do this you could have two directory windows open to display the contents of both directories *side-by-side*.

TO OPEN A SECOND DIRECTORY WINDOW

To open a second directory window, double-click on the drive's icon. Then, select the desired directory. Let's review the steps to open a second window.

1. Start by displaying one of the directories that you want to view—select the appropriate drive and directory.

2. Double-click on the icon of the drive containing the other directory, even if it is the same drive that has already been displayed.

A second window will appear overlapping the first. (See Figure 13.1.) If you selected the same drive, a duplicate of the first window will appear but the Title bar will indicate that the second window is the second instance, such as

C:\WINDOWS*.*:2

As an alternative, you can open a second instance of the current directory by selecting New Window from the Window menu. Notice that the Title bar of the directory window in the foreground appears in reverse, indicating it is the *active* directory window.

3. Select the desired directory in the tree.

A new directory window will be displayed with the same view options specified in the View menu of the first directory window. So if you selected to display only the tree and then opened a second window, the second window will also display just the tree. Once multiple directory windows are displayed, options in the View menu apply only to the active window. Changing the view options in the active window will not affect other inactive directory windows.

WORKING WITH MULTIPLE DIRECTORIES

You can switch, tile, cascade, move, or change the size of directory windows. For example, if you plan to copy files from one directory to another, you can maximize the File Manager window, and then change the size of the directory windows and move them so that they do not overlap each other.

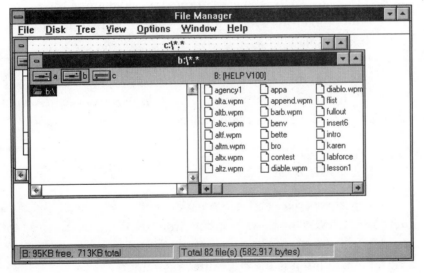

FIGURE 13.1:

Two directories shown in overlapping windows.

To tile the directory windows so they appear side-by-side, follow these steps:

1. Maximize the File Manager window. Click on the maximize button.

2. Hold down the shift key and select Tile from the Window menu. The directory windows will appear side-by-side, evenly dividing the File Manager window, as shown in Figure 13.2.

Note that if you do not hold down the shift key when you select Tile, the directory windows will appear stacked top and bottom rather than side-by-side.

In the lessons that follow, you will learn how to manipulate the files in the directory listing. Now exit File Manager and Windows. Even with multiple directory windows displayed, you can exit File Manager quickly by double-clicking on its Control box. You do not have to close the directory windows as a separate step.

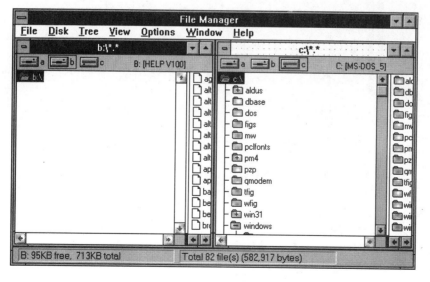

FIGURE 13.2:

Two directories shown side-by-side.

14 LESSON

Running Application Programs

n Lesson 7, you learned how to run a program that is shown as an icon in a group window. You can run a program, whether or not it is included in a group, from within Program Manager and File Manager. In this lesson, you'll learn how to run programs by selecting them in File Manager and by using the Run command in the File menu.

You will also learn two ways to run a program and open a document in one step. You can drag the document file to the application, or you can select a file whose extension has been associated with an application. In this lesson you will learn how to use these methods.

Running a Program from the Directory

There are several ways to run a program by selecting it in the directory contents list. You can run just the program itself and then open one of its documents, or you can run the program and open a document at the same time.

To run a program without opening a particular document, follow these steps:

1. Display the directory containing the file.

2. Double-click on the file name.

OPENING A DOCUMENT IN THE DIRECTORY

One way to start an application and open a document is to drag the document with the mouse to the application's start-up file name.

To do this, follow these steps:

1. Adjust the size of the directory window so that you can see both the names of the application's start-up file and the document you want to open.

2. Drag the document onto the application's start-up file name.

As you drag the mouse, a copy of the document's icon with a plus sign in its center will move with the pointer. As you move the icon, a selection box will appear surrounding the names of executable files that the icon passes over.

3. Move the icon until the selection box appears on the application's start-up file that you want to run, and then release the mouse button.

The File Manager will display a confirmation dialog box, similar to that shown in Figure 14.1.

4. Select Yes.

Windows will run the application and attempt to open the selected document into it. If the document is compatible with the program, the application will appear with the document. You will have no trouble using a document that was originally created with the application, or one in a format that the program recognizes.

However, your results will vary if you try opening a program with an incompatible document, such as dragging an executable program file to a word processing program. In some cases, the application may start but it will display a document window full of nonsense characters. If this occurs, exit the application and start over with a correct document. At other times, a warning message or dialog box may appear. Select OK to remove the dialog box and try again with a compatible document.

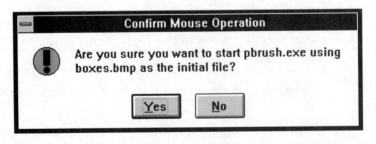

FIGURE 14.1:

The Confirm Mouse Operation dialog box prompts you for confirmation to run compatible applications.

BROWSING THROUGH FILES USING PROGRAM MANAGER

If you want to run a program but are not sure of the program's name or its directory, first activate the Program Manager window and select Run from Program Manager's File menu. (See Figure 14.2.) Then select Browse in the Run dialog box. Windows will display the Browse dialog box shown in Figure 14.3.

The executable program files in the current directory are shown in the File Name list box. Scroll the box if necessary, highlight the program that you want to run, and then select OK. The Run dialog box will reappear with the selected program name in the Command Line text box. Select OK to execute the program.

If the program you want to run is not in the list box of the Browse dialog box, select a new directory in the Directories list box, or change disk drives using the Drives text box and its drop-down list box.

By default, the File Name list box shows only executable files. To list all files, select List Files of Type, pull down the list box and select the All Files (*.*) option.

Running Applications with Documents

You can also run an application and open a specific document in one step by *associating* an extension with an application. The association tells Windows that files with a specific extension are documents of that application. When you "run" the document using either of the methods

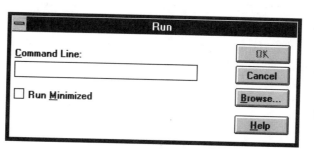

FIGURE 14.2:

The Run dialog box allows you to enter the name of an application to be executed.

previously explained for running a program, Windows will automatically start the application and open the selected document.

Certain associations are established by default when you install Windows. These are listed in Table 14.1. For example, if you double-click on a file with the TXT extension, Windows will execute the Notepad application and open the selected document.

In addition, on installation, most Windows applications will form the association with their default document file extension automatically. For instance, if you install PageMaker4, you can work on a Page-Maker publication by selecting a file with the PM4 extension.

To use this procedure with other document extensions, you must designate the association yourself. For example, you could associate PAS with a Pascal compiler or ACT with an accounting application.

To form an association, run File Manager, then follow these steps:

1. Highlight a document file. Make sure that the file format is compatible with the application.

2. Select Associate in the File menu. Windows will display a dialog box like that shown in Figure 14.4.

The extension of the selected file appears in the Files With Extension text box. If you did not highlight a file before displaying the dialog box, no extension will be shown—you must enter it before continuing.

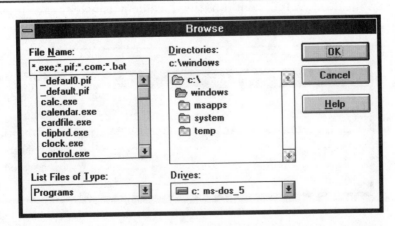

FIGURE 14.3:

The Browse dialog box allows you to select the application.

APPLICATION	EXTENSION
Calendar	CAL
Cardfile	CRD
Terminal	TRM
Notepad	TXT and INI
Paintbrush	BMP and PCX
Write	WRI
Recorder	REC

TABLE 14.1:

Default File Name Extensions for Application Program Associations

The Associate With list box describes file formats that are associated with Windows applications and accessory programs.

3. If the application is shown in the Associate With list box, select it. For example, to associate an extension with Windows Notepad, scroll down the list and select Text File (notepad.exe).

If the application is not listed, type the path and name of the program you want to associate with the extension in the Associate With text box. If necessary, use the Browse option to locate and insert the name.

4. Select OK.

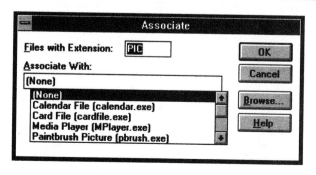

FIGURE 14.4:

The Associate dialog box links a document extension to an application program.

CHANGING AN ASSOCIATION

It may happen that several Windows applications will use the same document extension. When you install the applications, each would be associated with the same extension. Windows, however, will ignore all except the last association that was formed.

For example, suppose you install two word processing programs that both use the DOC file extension and then you select a document created with the first application. Windows will run the second word processing program and try to open the document into it. Because the file type of a document generated by the first application may be incompatible with the second application, you could receive an error message, see garbage on the screen, or even freeze your system.

If this occurs, you should change the association of this document back to the first application. Highlight a file with the DOC extension and then select Associate from the File menu. In the Associate With list box, select the name of the first word processing application you installed to associate it with the extension, and then select OK.

REMOVING AN ASSOCIATION

If you no longer want to associate an extension with an application, highlight a file with the extension, and then select Associate from the File menu. Select (None) under Associate With, and then select OK.

Program Type and Operating Mode

If you are using a computer that runs only Standard mode, or if you started Windows by typing WIN/S, a dialog box will appear on the screen if you try running a program that requires 386 Enhanced mode. Other than that, you should have no problem running any Windows application.

DOS applications may be a little trickier. If you are working in Standard mode, you can run only one DOS application at a time in full-screen. In Enhanced mode, you can run DOS applications in their own windows.

If Windows does not run a DOS program, or runs it incorrectly, you'll need a PIF file. A *Program Information File* gives Windows information on how to run a DOS application, such as special memory requirements. When you execute the PIF file, Windows uses the information to run the DOS program as efficiently as possible. Many DOS applications come with PIF files that you can transfer to the Windows directory. If you do not have a PIF file for a DOS application, Windows will use a file called Default.PIF.

Before running any DOS program, make sure that it is safe to run it under Windows. Programs that change the contents of directories, such as CHKDSK, should never be run from Windows, but only from the DOS prompt. This also applies to utility programs that undelete files or directories unless they are designed specifically to run within Windows. Check the program's manual to see if it is compatible with Windows. If you have any doubts, do not run it.

15 L E S S O N

Creating
directories

Sort directories

Limiting files
displayed

Changing file
attributes

▼

Working with Directories and File Attributes

ou should take advantage of the DOS directory structure by organizing your files into collections with a common theme. Keep each major application in its own directory, and use subdirectories to store your documents.

Once you plan your organization, you can create the directories and then copy your files into them. In this lesson you will learn how to create directories and how to customize the way files in the directory contents list are displayed on the screen. You'll also learn how to change file attributes to further organize your files and to protect your work.

How to Create a Directory

To create a directory directly from File Manager, follow these steps:

1. Run File Manager. In the directory tree, click once on the directory under which you want your new directory to appear.

For example, to create a directory branching from the root, click on the root directory in the tree. To create a subdirectory under Windows, click on the Windows directory.

2. In the File menu, select Create Directory. Windows displays the Create Directory dialog box. (See Figure 15.1.)

The path name of the highlighted directory will be the Current directory.

3. In the Name text box, type the name of the new directory. The new directory will become a branch of the current

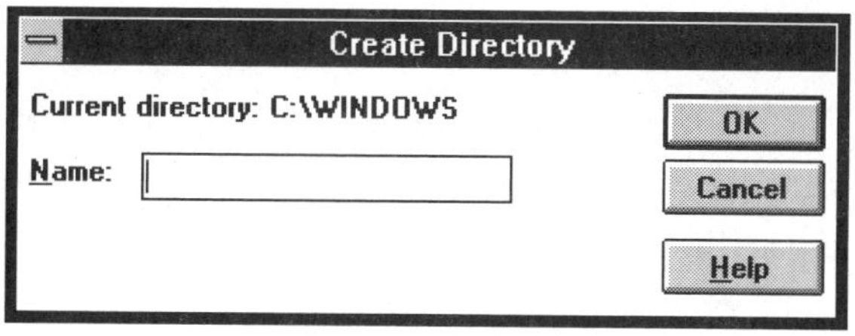

FIGURE 15.1:

The Create Directory dialog box permits you to make a new directory.

directory. If you selected the wrong directory in the tree, type the complete path name of the new directory, such as

C:\WP51\LETTERS

Then, the current directory will be ignored.

4. Select OK.

The new directory will now appear in the tree diagram.

How to Customize the Directory Contents List

Use the View drop-down menu to change the way files are displayed in the directory contents list. You can show additional details for each file, change the order of the files, or list specific types of files.

HOW TO LIST DETAILS ABOUT FILES

From the View menu in File Manager, select All File Details to display the size of each file in bytes, the date and time the file was last saved, and file attributes as shown in Figure 15.2. (You'll learn more about file attributes later in this lesson.)

To specify which details to list, select Partial Details from the View menu to see the Partial Details dialog box shown in Figure 15.3. Select the items that you want to display in the directory, and then select OK.

Changing the Default Values

The options that you select in this dialog box will only affect the active directory window. Note that if you want to use the custom settings for every directory, you must select Save Settings on Exit from the Options menu before you exit File Manager.

If you have several directory windows displayed, you can customize each one individually, showing just the names in one directory and additional details in another. Activate (click on) a window, then select your options in the View menu. To save new settings as the default, activate the directory window containing the settings you want to save before exiting File Manager.

To use the same settings on multiple directory windows, select the options you want for the first directory window, then open the other directory windows. The current directory window's settings are always the defaults for new directory windows.

HOW TO CHANGE THE ORDER IN WHICH FILES ARE LISTED IN A DIRECTORY

By default, File Manager displays file names in alphabetical order. To list files in another order, select the desired Sort By option in the View menu. In all of the arrangements, directories are always listed first, but they will be sorted according to the option selected.

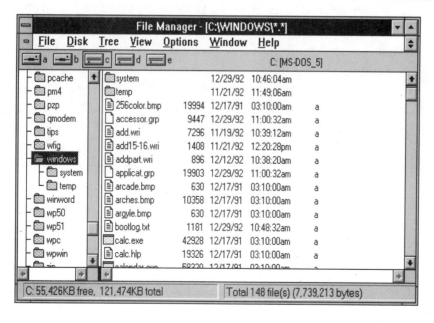

FIGURE 15.2:

Directory Contents list showing all file details.

- Sort by Name, the default, lists files by the ASCII values of their names, with those starting with numbers and punctuation marks first.

- Sort By Type lists files by their extension, arranged alphabetically. This is useful if you use standard extensions to identify types of files.

- Sort By Size lists the largest files first.

- Sort by Date list files by the date and time they were last saved. The most recent files are listed first.

HOW TO LIST SPECIFIC TYPES OF FILES

It may be easier to locate a specific file if you limit the directory display just to files of that type. To find a particular word processing document, for example, you could just list files with the DOC extension.

When deleting files from the directory, you should limit the files displayed. This may prevent you from accidentally deleting application programs or system files used by Windows. If you plan to purge a directory of unwanted document files, for instance, make sure to list just the files associated with the application, not the application itself.

To limit the files, select By File Type in the View menu to display the dialog box shown in Figure 15.4.

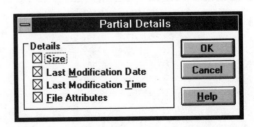

FIGURE 15.3:

The Partial Details dialog box provides options of file displaying details.

To Specify a Group of Files

The default entry in the Name text box, *.* in the By File Type dialog box, indicates that you want to list files with any name and any extension. The asterisks are *wildcards* that represent any text string on both sides of the period.

You can designate files manually by entering names, extensions, or wildcards in the text box. For example, to list just Word for Windows document files, enter *.DOC in the text box and select OK. The wildcard tells File Manager to list all files with the DOC extension.

The question mark (?) is another wildcard, but it represents a single character. Entering *.?IF, for instance, would list files with extensions that end in IF, such as PIF and TIF.

Listing Files by Type

The check boxes under File Type in the By File Type dialog box will list the files in the manner explained in Table 15.1.

The two options, Programs and Documents, provide a way to display files which represent similar types of files but with several different extensions. Using the Name text box, for example, you can list only program files with a single extension, i.e., COM, EXE, PIF, or BAT—using wildcards such as *.COM. When you select the file type Programs, however, you can list all executable files in the directory.

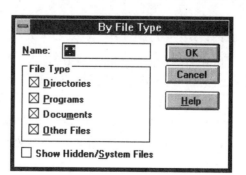

FIGURE 15.4:

The By File Type dialog box allows you to specify what types of files to display.

FILE TYPE	CORRESPONDING FILES
Directories	Subdirectories only
Programs	Files with the extensions COM, EXE, BAT, and PIF
Documents	Files with extensions associated with the applications in the directory
Other Files	Files not included in the other categories

TABLE 15.1:

File Type Distinguished By File Manager

Note that using the Documents file type is different from manually entering *.DOC in the Name text box. Although *.DOC lists only files with the DOC extension, the Documents option shows every file that has an extension associated with an application.

By combining wildcards and file types, you can select specific groups of files. For example, entering BUDGET.* in the Name box and selecting Documents will list word processing, graphic, and all other document files that are named "budget."

Specifying an extension in the Name text box will not override the selections in the File Type check boxes. If you enter *.DOC in the Name text box and check only the program's check box, no files will be listed, just the message

No files found.

will appear in the directory contents list.

Listing Hidden and System Files

There are files on your disk that will not be listed in the directory automatically. Usually these are files needed for your operating system to boot your computer. Windows does not display these files in order to prevent you from accidentally deleting or renaming them. If you did delete or rename them, you wouldn't be able to start your computer.

Technically, these are files with either the Hidden or the System attribute set. You'll learn about attributes, and how to change them later in this lesson.

If you do want to list these files, select Show Hidden/System Files in the By File Type dialog box. Hidden files are always displayed with a document icon that has an exclamation point (!). This icon is a warning not to tamper with these files.

How to Change File Attributes

For each file, DOS stores special information, called file attributes, to control the types of operations that you can perform on the file. By changing the attributes, you can protect files from being deleted, modified, or even displayed in the directory.

A file's current attributes are shown in the directory listing when you select either All File Details from the View menu or File Attributes from the Partial Details dialog box. The attributes, and the letters used to represent them, are listed in Table 15.2.

To change an attribute, highlight the file you wish to change and then press Alt-↵ or select Properties from the File menu. File Manager will display the dialog box shown in Figure 15.5.

The dialog box shows the file name, size, the date it was last saved, and path. Its current attributes are shown with the X's in check boxes. Select the attributes that you want to assign or remove, and then select OK.

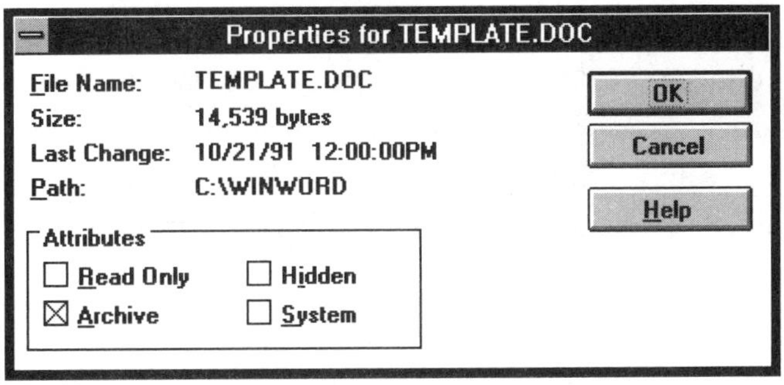

FIGURE 15.5:

The Properties dialog box is used to change file attributes.

Properties for TEMPLATE.DOC

File Name: TEMPLATE.DOC
Size: 14,539 bytes
Last Change: 10/21/91 12:00:00PM
Path: C:\WINWORD

OK
Cancel
Help

Attributes
☐ Read Only   ☐ Hidden
☒ Archive   ☐ System

DESIGNATOR	ATTRIBUTE
A	Archive identifies for BACKUP or XCOPY command that a file has been changed since the last formal backup operation and therefore needs to be saved during a backup operation.
H	Hidden prevents a file from being listed in the directory.
R	Read-Only prevents a file from being changed, renamed, or deleted.
S	System identifies files used by DOS.

TABLE 15.2:

DOS File Attributes

SYSTEM FILES

Do not remove the System and Read-Only attributes from DOS system files. If you did, you could accidentally change or delete the files and then not be able to restart your computer. You can't harm system files by removing the Hidden attributes. Because the System attribute is specific to DOS, avoid setting this attribute for your own files.

READ-ONLY FILES

Use the Read-Only attribute to protect a file from being changed or deleted. With this attribute set, you can run, display, or print a file but you cannot overwrite or delete it. If you do want to alter or erase the file later, use the Change Attribute dialog box to remove the read-only status.

Most word processing programs allow you to open a read-only file and to make changes to it on-screen. However, they will not allow you to save the edited file under the same name. If this occurs and you want to save the changes, you must save the file under a different name. Then, you can remove the Read-only attribute from the original file so that you can delete it. Rename the edited file and set the Read-only attribute again.

HIDDEN FILES

To protect a file from prying eyes, you can add the Hidden attribute. Anyone with access to your system and Windows, however, can still display the file by choosing the Show Hidden/System Files in the By File Type dialog box. You can also run a hidden file by typing its name in the Run dialog box, or by selecting its icon if it has been added to a group.

If you mark a file as hidden, make sure that *you* remember that the file exists. If you do not select to display hidden files, over time, you might forget that the file is in the directory.

Once you designate a file as hidden, you'll have to select Show Hidden/System Files if you want to change its attributes later.

ARCHIVE FILES

When you change a file, or create a new one, DOS automatically turns on the Archive attribute, indicating that the file needs to be backed up. When you back up your disk, you can tell the DOS BACKUP command and most third-party backup programs, to record only files with the attribute turned on. After the backup is made, most programs will turn off the Archive attribute so that the file is not backed up again unless it is modified.

Prior to making the backup, you can save time and disk space by turning off the Archive attribute for files that you do not need to save. For example, there is no need to back up application programs if you already have copies of the original disks on which they were supplied.

Searching for Files
and Directories

Finding a specific file can be troublesome even when your computer has the capability to display multiple directories. You can use File Manager's Search function, however, to locate a file, or a directory quickly, no matter where it is on the disk, rather than opening directories to list files.

The Search function is especially useful when you have related documents in different directories. For instance, suppose you have a budget spreadsheet file called BUDGET.XLS in the Excel directory, a graphic file called BUDGET.PCX in the Windows directory, and a budget report called BUDGET.DOC in the Winword directory. To locate all of the files quickly, you could tell the Search function to search for BUDGET.*, and all three files would be found in a very short time.

What if you had a number of unrelated files with the same name, such as LETTER, but they were in different directories. How could you locate the file that you want? If you tried to locate LETTER by opening and displaying different directories, you might not realize that several different versions of the specific file you want exist, and you might recall the incorrect document. The Search command, however, will display all files with the name LETTER, so you can then determine which file you want to recall.

Using the Search Command

When you want to locate a file or directory using Search, follow these steps:

1. Start File Manager.

2. If you want to search a specific directory, select the directory in the tree. To search the entire disk, select the root directory. Although you will be able to specify a directory in the Search dialog box, when you select the directory first, it saves you the trouble of having to type a path later.

3. Pull down the File menu and select Search to display the Search dialog box shown in Figure 16.1.

If a file was highlighted in the directory list, the Search For text box will use its extension, such as *.DOC, as the default. So to search for all files with a specific extension, select one of the files before starting Search. If no file is highlighted, the text box will display *.*.

4. In the Search For text box, type the name of the file or directory which you are trying to locate. Use wildcards to locate a group of files with a common name or extension.

5. The name of the selected directory in the tree appears in the Start From text box. If you want to search another directory, enter its path. For instance, if you initiated Search when a subdirectory was selected, enter C:\ in the text box to search the entire disk.

6. By default, File Manager will search all subdirectories beginning at the Start From path. If you selected the root directory, the search will include the entire disk. To search just the Start From directory and none of its subdirectories, select the Search All Subdirectories check box to remove the X from the check box.

7. Select OK.

Windows will search the specified directories and then open a Search Results window showing the complete path of each located file or directory. (See Figure 16.2.) You can run programs in the Search window as you would in any other directory, and you can move, copy, or print listed files as you'll learn how to do in later lessons.

Close the window with the Control box when you no longer need it to be open.

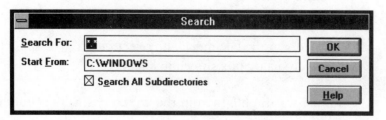

FIGURE 16.1:

The Search dialog box prompts you for the search path and file name.

If Search cannot locate the file, you will see a dialog box with the message

No matching files were found.

Select OK to return to File Manager.

SEARCHING PARTITIONS

If your hard disk is divided into more than one partition, or logical drive, only the current partition will be searched. For instance, if your hard disk is split into drives C and D, and the C drive is the current drive, only drive C will be searched. To search for a file on drive D, you must first activate that drive in File Manager.

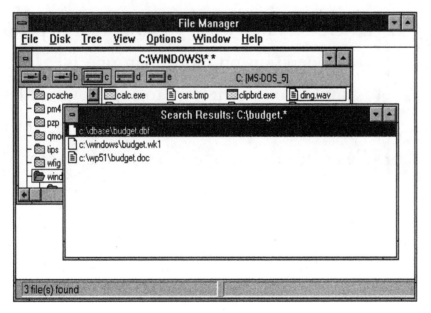

FIGURE 16.2:

The Search Results window displays all matching items found in the search path.

FEATURING

Selecting
consecutive and
nonconsecutive
files
Deselecting files
▼

Selecting Files

There are times when you will want to perform an operation on more than one file. For example, you might want to copy several files to a floppy disk, or to delete a number of unwanted files at one time. In the lessons that follow, you will learn how to delete, move, copy, and otherwise manipulate several files at a time. You will begin this lesson by learning how to *select* more than one file at a time.

Note that although all of the instructions in this lesson refer to *files*, they apply equally well to directories. You can select multiple directories at one time, and even select a combination of files and directories.

To Select Files Listed Consecutively

When you want to select several files that are listed in a row, follow these steps:

1. Point to the first file of the group and click the left mouse button.

2. Move the pointer to the last file of the group and hold down the Shift key while you click the mouse button.

To Select Nonconsecutive Files

To select files that are not listed consecutively, select the first file, then press and hold the Ctrl key and click on any other files that you want to select.

To Select Groups of Consecutive Files

Follow these steps when you want to select several different groups of files:

1. Point to the first file of the group and click the left mouse button.

2. Move the pointer to the last file of the group and hold down the Shift key while you click the mouse button.

3. To select the next group of files, press and hold down the Ctrl key and click on the first file of the group.

4. Press Ctrl-Shift, and click on the last file of the group.

Selecting Files with a Dialog Box

The Select Files dialog box shown in Figure 17.1 allows you to select related groups of files quickly, even when the files are not listed consecutively.

When you want to select files with the Select Files dialog box, follow these steps:

1. Select Select Files from the File menu.

By default, the dialog box is set to select every file in the directory by the entry *.* in the File[s] text box.

2. To select a single file, type its name into the File[s] text box. To select a group of related files use wildcards, such as *.PCX for all files with the PCX extension.

3. Choose Select. The designated files will be highlighted in the directory contents list but the Select Files dialog box will remain on the screen.

Note that once you make a selection, the Cancel button changes to a Close button.

4. Repeat steps 2 and 3 to select any additional files. For additional files, the dialog box works as if the Ctrl key was held down.

When you make a selection, that does not cancel any other selections that you have made. In this way you can select groups of files that do not have a name or an extension in common. After selecting all PCX files, for example, you can select all TIF files (*.TIF) or any other types of files.

5. When you have finished selecting files, choose Close.

The Select Files dialog box will close and the directory window will have the selected files highlighted.

SELECTING THE ENTIRE DIRECTORY

To select all of the files in the directory contents list with the keyboard, use the Tab key to make sure that the cursor is in the directory contents list and then press Ctrl-/ (Slash). With the mouse, you have to select the files as one consecutive group, as explained previously, or use the Select Files dialog box as described above.

To Deselect a Specific File

To deselect a single file from a group of selected files, point to the file, hold down the Ctrl key and click the left mouse button.

To Deselect a Group of Files

To deselect several files at one time, display the Select Files dialog box. Enter the name of a file you wish to deselect, or use wildcards to designate a group of files. Then click on the Deselect button.

Repeat the process to deselect other groups or files, and then choose Close to return to the directory window.

TO DESELECT ALL SELECTED FILES

To deselect all of the highlighted files, choose Select Files from the File menu, then click on the Deselect button.

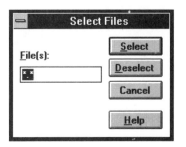

FIGURE 17.1:

The Select Files dialog box allows you to select groups of files.

18 LESSON

Copying and Moving Files and Directories

In this lesson you will learn how to copy a file and/or directory, and how to move it from one location to another.

When you move or copy a file with the mouse, Windows will display a Confirm Mouse Operations dialog box, as shown in Figure 18.1. This is to safeguard against accidentally moving or copying a file. Select Yes to continue the operation or No to cancel it.

If your destination (target) directory already contains a file with the same name as the one you are copying or moving, File Manager will display a Confirm File Replace dialog box. (See Figure 18.2.) Select Yes to replace the existing file with the file being copied or moved. If there are several duplicate file names, each will have its own Confirm File Replace dialog box—select Yes or No for each one. To replace all of the files without being prompted for each one, select Yes to All.

If a floppy diskette fills up while you are moving or copying files onto it, Windows will display a dialog box similar to the one shown in Figure 18.3. Insert another diskette into the drive and select Retry, or select Cancel to abort the operation.

To Make a Copy of a File or Directory

When you copy a file or directory, you make a duplicate of it. The original file or directory remains intact. Note that when you copy a directory, you copy all of the files and subdirectories contained within it in one step. You can copy files and directories at the same time by highlighting their icons and then moving the whole selection.

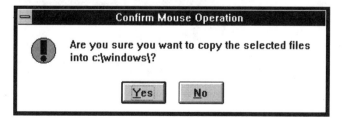

FIGURE 18.1:

File Manager displays the Confirm Mouse Operation dialog box to prevent accidentally moving or copying a file.

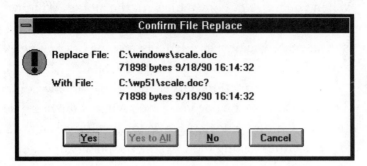

FIGURE 18.2:

File Manager displays a Confirm File Replace dialog box when an operation will overwrite an existing file or directory.

COPYING FILES ON A SINGLE DRIVE

How you copy files or directories depends on whether you copy them to a directory on the same disk drive, or from one disk drive to another. To copy a file or directory on the same drive, follow these steps:

1. Start File Manager and display the directory containing the file or directory you want to copy. Make sure that both the directory tree and the directory contents list appear in the directory window.

FIGURE 18.3:

The Error Copying File dialog box appears when a floppy diskette becomes full during a copy or move operation.

2. In the directory contents list, highlight the file or directory that you want to copy. To copy multiple files or directories, highlight them as you learned to do in Lesson 17.

If you can see in the directory tree both the directory you want to copy (the source directory) and the directory you want to move it to (the target directory), highlight the source directory and then skip to step 4.

3. If you cannot see the name of the target directory in the directory tree, use the scroll bar to display the directory's name. Double-click on the source directory to open its own directory window.

4. Press and hold the Ctrl key, then click on the highlighted file or source directory and drag your selection onto the destination (target) directory. The mouse pointer will change into a file or directory icon with a plus sign (+). The plus sign indicates that you are copying, not moving, a file. When you are copying multiple files, the pointer will look like several icons overlapping.

Note that if you drag the icon into an area where you cannot copy the files, the icon will change into a slashed circle. For example, you cannot copy the files into the Program Manager window or onto the desktop.

5. When a selection box appears around the target directory, release both the mouse button and the Ctrl key. File Manager will then display the Confirm Mouse Operation dialog box.

6. Select Yes to copy the files, or No to cancel the operation.

Windows will display a dialog box showing the source and destination paths of each file as it is being copied. To stop the procedure, select Cancel in the dialog box.

COPYING FILES TO ANOTHER DRIVE

To copy a file or directory to another drive, select the files as explained previously, and then drag the selection to the disk drive icon under the Menu bar. Note that you do not have to hold down the Ctrl key while you are dragging the selection.

When you copy a file to another drive by dragging the file onto the drive icon, the file will be placed in the drive's root directory. To place it in another directory, you must open *two* directory windows. Display the directory window that contains the files you want to copy from (the source directory) and the directory you want to copy the files to (the target directory). Tile or size the windows so that both are displayed, as you learned in Lesson 10. Select the files that you want to copy and then drag the icon onto the destination directory in the other window.

To Move a File or Directory

When you have finished working with a document or other file, you may want to remove it from your hard disk. However, you should keep an archived copy of that document or file in case you need it at some later date.

When you move a directory, you move all of the files and subdirectories contained within it. You can move files and directories at the same time by highlighting their icons and then moving the whole selection.

The procedure for moving a file or directory is almost identical to copying. Follow the steps given for copying a file but press and hold down the Alt key instead of the Ctrl key. To move a file or directory to another location on the same drive, however, you do not have to press the Alt key.

Table 18.1 summarizes the methods to copy and move files.

MOVING OR COPYING A FILE WITHIN THE SAME DRIVE:	
WHEN ...	PRESS AND HOLD ...
Copying	Ctrl key and left mouse button
Moving	Left mouse button alone
MOVING OR COPYING A FILE TO A DIFFERENT DRIVE:	
WHEN ...	PRESS ...
Copying	Left mouse button alone
Moving	Alt key and left mouse button

TABLE 18.1:

Summary of Methods to Copy and Move Files

Turning Off the Confirmation Box

The confirmation boxes are provided as a valuable safeguard against *accidentally* replacing an existing file with the Copy or Move commands. If you find it tiresome to confirm each operation, however, you can turn off the dialog boxes to save time.

1. Select Confirmation from the File Manager Options menu. The Confirmation dialog box shown in Figure 18.4 will appear.

These options let you choose during which operation(s) you want the Confirmation box to appear, as shown in Table 18.2. By default they are set so the dialog box appears with each operation.

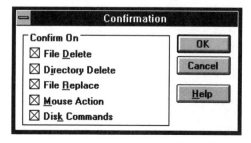

FIGURE 18.4:

The Confirmation dialog box allows you to turn confirmation boxes on or off.

OPTION	OPERATION
File Delete	File Manager will display a dialog box for each file that you select to delete. (See Lesson 20 for a discussion on deleting files.)
Directory Delete	File Manager will display a dialog box for each directory that you delete.
File Replace	File Manager will display a dialog box for each file you move or copy that would overwrite an existing file.
Mouse Action	File Manager will display a dialog box before moving or copying when you drag files with a mouse.
Disk Commands	File Manager will display a dialog box before formatting or copying a disk. Diskette operations are discussed in Lesson 21.

TABLE 18.2:
Confirmation Options

2. Click on the option to remove the X in its check box, turning off the option. Click again to turn it back on.

3. Select OK.

To save your changes, select Save Settings on Exit from the Options menu before quitting File Manager.

Renaming Files and Directories

fter copying a file from one directory to another, you will probably want to change its name. That way, you will not have two files with the same name. Also, you may want to create a file in a directory and use a name that you have already assigned. In such a case, you should rename the original file before using that name for the second file.

In this lesson, you will learn how File Manager lets you rename files, directories, and even subdirectories.

Caution: Do not change the names of Windows' own system files or directories. If you do, Windows will be unable to locate the files it needs to function.

To Change the Name of a File

When you want to change the name of a file, follow these steps:

1. Select the file.

2. Select Rename from File Manager's File menu to display the Rename dialog box. (See Figure 19.1.)

3. Enter a new file name in the To text box. To rename a file other than the one selected, enter its name in the From text box.

4. Select OK.

If you enter a new path or directory name in the To text box, File Manager will display a warning box. To rename a file and place it in another directory in one step, use the Move option in the File menu.

If a file with the same name already exists in the destination (target) directory, the confirmation dialog box will appear.

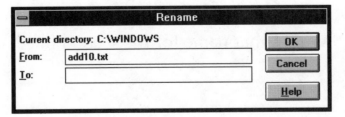

FIGURE 19.1:

The Rename dialog box lets you change a file name.

RENAMING MULTIPLE FILES

You cannot rename more than one file at a time, unless you simply want to change their extensions. For example, suppose you want to change the extension of several files to .BAK. Select the files, then choose Rename from the File Menu and enter *.BAK in the To text box. File Manager will rename the files using their original names but with the new extension.

To Change the Name of a Directory

Windows allows you to change the name of a directory as easily as you can rename a file. Select the directory you want to rename in either the directory tree or the directory contents list. Then select Rename from the File menu. Type the directory's new name in the To text box, and then select OK.

Be careful when changing directory names. If the name of the directory was used in a batch (BAT) or a PIF file, both DOS and Windows will be unable to locate the directory at the appropriate time. They will look for a directory with the original name. So, if you change the name of a directory used in a BAT or PIF file, you have to change all of the references to it in your other BAT or PIF files.

FEATURING

Deleting directories that contain files

▼

Deleting Files and Directories

Deleting a file removes it from the disk. Although there are some utility programs that may be able to restore a deleted file, there are no guarantees that you can always get the file back again. In fact, do not run an undelete utility unless it is designed specifically for Windows. If it is not specific to Windows, the program may undelete the file but it also may leave the disk's directory damaged and useless.

Never delete a file unless you are absolutely sure you won't need it again, or unless you have copied it on another diskette. For example, do not routinely delete word processing documents just because you've printed and distributed the documents. You might need to recall a file at some later time to print another copy; to make changes to it for updating purposes; or to use parts of it in some other document.

Windows' delete command is more powerful than either the Delete or Erase command in DOS. The DOS commands allow you to delete only a single file or a group of related files using the wildcards * and ?. With wildcards, you can erase all files in the same directory that have the same name or extension, or some characters in common; for example, Budget*.9* would erase all Budget documents with extensions starting with 9. But you cannot use wildcards to delete a series of files that are listed consecutively with totally different file names in the directory, or a number of unrelated files with one command.

With Windows, you can delete *any group* of highlighted files in the directory contents list. Windows also allows you to delete a directory or subdirectory, even if it contains files. With DOS, you must first delete all of the files in a directory before you can delete the directory.

To Delete a File
When you want to delete a file, follow these steps:

1. Select the file or files you want to delete.

2. Press the Del key, or select Delete from the File menu in File Manager, to display a Delete dialog box similar to the one shown in Figure 20.1.

The name of the selected file will be highlighted in the Delete text box. If you are deleting multiple files, File Manager will list as many file names as possible in the dialog box, although *all* of the selected files will be deleted if you continue.

To delete a file other than the one shown, enter its name in the Delete text box.

3. Select OK to display the Confirm File Delete dialog box. (See Figure 20.2.)

Remember, you can turn off the confirmation box, as explained in Lesson 18, but if you do, you will lose an important safeguard against possible disaster.

4. Select Yes to delete the file, No to skip it and go on to the next highlighted file, if any, or Cancel to stop the procedure. To delete multiple files without being prompted, select Yes to All.

How to Delete a Directory

Deleting a directory will delete all of the files and any subdirectories in that branch automatically.

To delete a directory, highlight its name in the directory tree or the directory contents list and then proceed as if you were deleting a file.

If you did not turn off the confirmation boxes, you will be prompted before each file and subdirectory is deleted. A Confirm

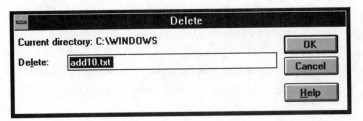

FIGURE 20.1:

The Delete dialog box allows you to delete single or multiple files.

Directory Delete dialog box or a Confirm File Delete dialog box will appear, depending on what you chose to be deleted. Selecting No in these Confirm Delete dialog boxes will cancel the operation. If you select Yes to All, every subdirectory and file will be deleted, without any further prompts. Therefore you should be very cautious when selecting Yes to All.

FIGURE 20.2:

The Confirm File Delete dialog box warns you against accidentally deleting files.

FEATURING

Copying floppy diskettes

Formatting diskettes

Changing the diskette labels

Making bootable system diskettes

▼

Working with Diskettes

In the previous lessons you learned how to use File Manager to manipulate files and directories. File Manager also gives you the capability of manipulating disks using the Disk menu. (See Figure 21.1.)

Each option on this menu has an equivalent DOS command. However, once you've started Windows it is far more convenient to remain in Windows to perform these functions than to use DOS. For example, instead of exiting Windows to format or copy a disk, just start File Manager and select the Format Disk or Copy Disk option from the Disk menu.

In this lesson, you will learn how to use File Manager to make copies of floppy diskettes; to change a disk's label; to format diskettes; and to make a system disk that can be used to boot your computer. (If you want to learn how to copy disks using DOS, see Appendix A.)

To Make Copies of Your Floppy Diskettes

All floppy diskettes can become so damaged that their files become unusable. Even the 3½-inch size in the rigid plastic case can be badly damaged. For this reason, you should make backup copies of all of your important diskettes *before* using them.

The Copy Disk option on the Disk menu makes an exact duplicate of a diskette. It will automatically erase any files that might be on the destination (target) diskette, or it will format a blank diskette. Note that although you will be warned that the contents of the destination diskette will be erased, you should first make sure that you are using either a diskette you no longer need or a blank one.

The Copy Disk option can make a copy of a diskette only to one that is the same size and format. For example, it cannot copy a 5¼-inch diskette to a 3½-inch one; nor can it copy the contents of a 1.44MB 3½-inch diskette to a 720K one of the same size. If you want to copy

FIGURE 21.1:

File Manager's Disk menu allows you to manipulate disks.

the entire contents of a diskette to a different type of diskette, you must use the Copy command in the File menu using the techniques that you learned in Lesson 18.

When you want to copy a diskette, follow these steps:

1. Insert the source diskette into a floppy disk drive.

2. Start File Manager and click on the drive icon containing the diskette that you want to copy, or press Ctrl and the drive letter. You can also press F6 or Tab to move the cursor to the drive icon area, and then use the arrow keys to select the drive.

3. Select the Copy Disk option from the Disk drop-down menu.

4. If your computer has two disk drives, the Copy Disk dialog box will appear. (See Figure 21.2.) Enter the source and destination (target) drives in the appropriate text boxes, and then select OK. If your disk drives are not the same size, enter the same drive name in both text boxes.

5. A dialog box appears asking you to confirm the operation. Select Yes to proceed. Otherwise, select No to cancel the Disk copy operation.

6. A dialog box appears telling you to insert the source disk. Select OK.

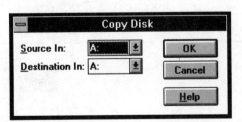

FIGURE 21.2:

The Copy Disk dialog box allows you to select source and destination drives.

While you are copying a diskette in one drive, you'll be prompted to swap the source and destination diskettes in and out of the drive at the appropriate times. Insert the diskette when prompted and then select OK.

As the diskette is copied, a dialog box will display the percentage of the copy operation that has been completed. You can discontinue the operation at any time by selecting Cancel. However, if you cancel the copy procedure before the diskette is completely copied, you will abort the operation. The target diskette that you were making the copy on will not be usable until you format it or complete another copy operation on it.

How to Assign a Disk Label

A disk or volume label is a name that you assign to identify a disk. Disk labels are particularly useful for managing floppy diskettes, especially if you group the files on your diskettes around a common theme. The label appears to the right of the drive icon area when the directory window is showing the contents of a diskette. It will help you to identify the diskette's contents very quickly.

To label a diskette, follow these steps:

1. Start File Manager and select the drive containing the diskette that you want to label.

2. Select the Label Disk option from the Disk drop-down menu. The Label Disk dialog box will appear. (See Figure 21.3.)

3. In the Label text box, type a label of not more than 11 characters.

4. Select OK.

How to Format a Disk

Unless you purchase diskettes that are preformatted, you cannot use a brand new diskette until you format it. Formatting a diskette prepares it electronically for use on your computer, dividing it into tracks and sectors that store your programs and files.

Note that if you reformat a diskette that already contains files, the files will be permanently erased.

To format new diskette, follow these steps:

1. Insert the diskette that you want to format into a disk drive.

2. Select Format Disk from the Disk menu. File Manager displays the Format Disk dialog box shown in Figure 21.4.

3. Select the drive containing the diskette that you want to format from the Disk In drop-down list box.

4. Select the capacity of the disk from the Capacity drop-down list box.

5. Choose any of the options desired. The options are listed in Table 21.1.

6. Select OK. A confirmation dialog box appears.

7. Make sure the disk drive contains a diskette that you want to format, and then select Yes.

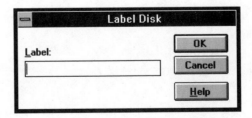

FIGURE 21.3:

The Label Disk dialog box allows you to label your diskettes.

OPTION	FUNCTION
Label	Enter an optional volume label, of no more than 11 characters.
Make System Disk	When the diskette is formatted, Windows copies the necessary files to allow you to use the diskette to start your computer. If you do not select this option, you can use the diskette to store files, but not to boot your system.
Quick Format	Select this option to reformat a disk that has already been formatted. This saves time by deleting the directory information from the diskette without scanning it for bad sectors. Do not select this option if the diskette has never been formatted, or if DOS has had trouble reading information on it.

TABLE 21.1:

Format Disk Options

How to Make a System Disk

If your hard disk becomes damaged, you may need a bootable floppy diskette to start your computer. This is a diskette that contains the system files your computer needs to load and start DOS. These system files are always stored on specific parts of the diskette. If you have a formatted nonbootable diskette with these locations unused, you can make

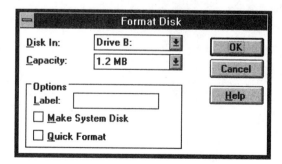

FIGURE 21.4:

The Format Disk dialog box contains several disk formatting options.

it bootable by selecting the Make System Disk option from File Manager's Disk menu. To do this, follow these steps:

1. Select the drive icon for the drive that contains the system files. Usually, this is drive C.

2. Insert the floppy diskette to which you want to add the system files.

3. Pull down the Disk menu and select the Make System Disk option.

4. If your computer has two disk drives, you will be prompted to select the destination drive. Select the letter of the drive which contains the floppy diskette.

5. Select OK. A confirmation dialog box will appear.

6. Select Yes.

Windows will display a System Disk Error dialog box if the reserved system file location on the diskette is taken by some other files. Select OK in the dialog box to cancel the operation. Because the system files must be placed in a *specific* location, you may have a relatively empty diskette but still be unable to make it into a system disk.

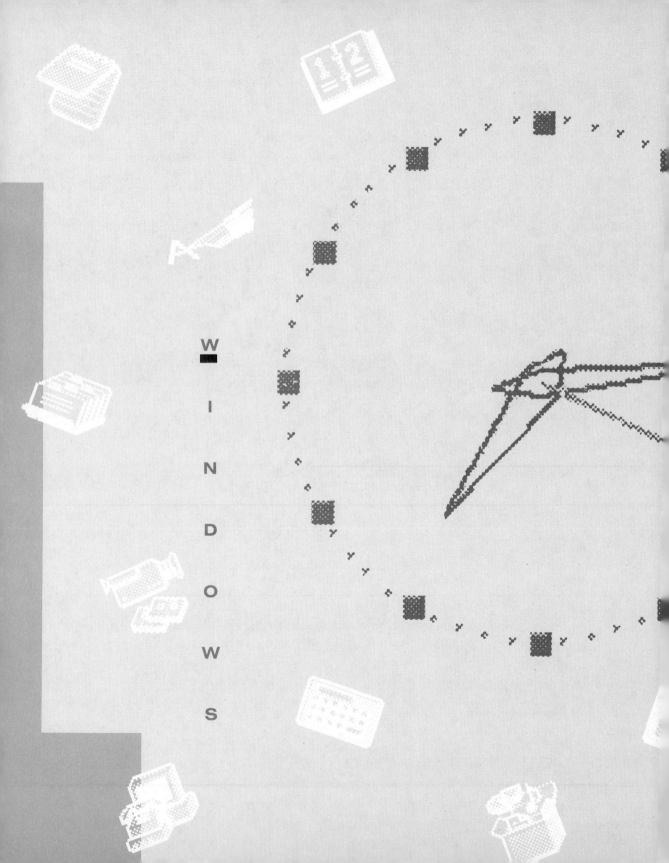

W
I
N
D
O
W
S

PART 4

The Accessories

In Lesson 3 you learned that Windows refers to the video screen as the desktop because you can arrange your work on the computer screen as you would on your office desk. Windows takes the concept even further by providing a set of office tools like those you probably keep on your desk, including a calculator, calendar, notepad, and clock. These tools are included among other useful programs in the Accessories group.

The lessons in Part 4 explain how to use all of Windows' accessories except Packager. (Packager is a more advanced program, designed for embedding items within other applications, and it is beyond the scope of this book.)

Introducing Desktop Accessories and Utilities

To use the tools in the Accessories group, you must first open its group window. When you first start Windows, the Main group window will appear. Below the window you will see the icons for the Accessories and Games groups.

How to Access the Accessories Group

In Lesson 7 you learned how to open the Accessories group by double-clicking on its icon. Using the keyboard, you press Ctrl-Tab until the icon is selected, and then press ↵. You can also select Accessories from the Window drop-down menu.

Once the Accessories window is open, you can run any accessory as you learned how to do in Lesson 7.

The Games Group

When you need some time off from work, take a look at the two programs in the Games group, Solitaire and Minesweeper. Solitaire is an electronic version of the popular card game; Minesweeper is a logic and strategy game in which you find your way through a mine field.

To play a game, open the Games group by double-clicking on the Games icon. Note that you won't find any information on the games in Windows' printed documentation. Instead, you can use each game's own Help feature after you begin running the game.

Both games have nothing to do with work productivity, but you may find that if you are having difficulties concentrating, playing a game may refresh your mind so that you can return to work with renewed vigor and interest.

Starting Accessories Automatically

If you find yourself using the same Accessory programs during most of your Windows sessions, you can set up the programs as pop-up utilities. A *pop-up utility* is a program such as the Calculator or Calendar that activates automatically when Windows starts.

To have an Accessory program activate itself automatically, you have to add it to the StartUp group. Working with groups is discussed in Lesson 31. You'll find instructions there for making pop-up utilities of Accessory programs.

Using Windows Clock

Although the Clock is one of the simplest desktop accessories that comes with Windows, it is also one of the most useful. When you are facing a deadline, or keeping track of the time you spend on particular tasks for billing purposes, you can display the time and date in their own window.

Here's how to use the Clock:

1. You run the Clock by double-clicking on its icon in the Accessories group window. Windows displays a small window with a digital clock that shows the time and date.

2. Select Settings from the Clock menu to display the drop-down menu shown in Figure 23.1.

3. Select Analog from the drop-down menu to change the display to an analog clock, as shown in Figure 23.2.

FIGURE 23.1:

You can change the Clock's appearance by choosing options from the Clock Settings drop-down menu.

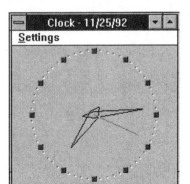

FIGURE 23.2:

You can change the display setting to show this Analog Clock.

The other options in the drop-down menu are as follows:

Set Font   Changes the font used to display the date and
time.

No Title   Removes the Title bar and Menu bar, leaving only
the clock in the window. To turn the Menu bar and
Title back on, double-click in the Clock window.

Seconds   Turns off the display of seconds in the digital
clock and the sweep seconds hand in the
analog clock.

Date   Turns off the display of the date.

To display the time while you're working, minimize the Clock window, and then arrange your other windows to make the Clock visible. (See Figure 23.3.) Note that the Clock may pause momentarily when

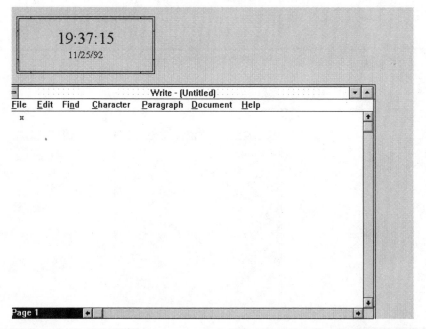

FIGURE 23.3:

The Clock (without Title and Menu bar, and in a different font) reduced and moved to stay on-screen while you work with another application.

you are performing some complex operation, but it will catch up when the operation is done.

You can also minimize the Clock to an icon. Unlike other programs that have picture icons when minimized, the Clock icon is an actual running clock that shows the correct time.

When you close the Clock window, its position and setting are saved in a file called CLOCK.INI. Windows uses this file to position the Clock the next time it is opened. To return to the default position, delete the CLOCK.INI file. Make sure that you do **not** delete CLOCK.EXE.

24 L E S S O N

FEATURING

Standard and scientific modes

Copying calculations to other applications

Performing statistical analyses

▼

Using the Windows Calculator

I t is ironic that although many users work with sophisticated computers, they still have to reach for their calculators when they need to perform some math calculations. This is not the case with Windows.

Windows Calculator program provides both a Standard and a Scientific calculator. Each has its own window that can be popped into view at any time. You can even copy the results of a calculation into another application such as a word processor.

Using the Standard Calculator

To display the Standard calculator, shown in Figure 24.1, double-click on the Calculator icon in the Accessories group window.

Notice that the Calculator window does not have maximize or restore buttons, and that its borders are composed of single lines unlike the double-line borders in other windows. Although you can move the Calculator window on the screen and minimize it to an icon, you cannot resize it manually.

You can activate a Calculator button by clicking it with the mouse. Using the mouse, you click on *each* number to enter it. With the keyboard, you can use either the number keys along the top of your keyboard or the numeric keypad on the right. If you press numbers on the keypad but none appears in the Calculator's display box, press the key labelled Num Lock. (To use the keys for cursor movements later, press Num Lock again.) Table 24.1 shows the keystrokes to use for nonnumeric buttons.

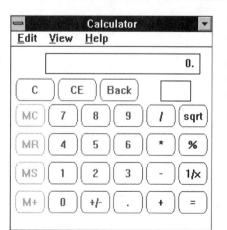

FIGURE 24.1:

The Standard calculator works the same way as your desk calculator.

BUTTON	KEYSTROKE	FUNCTION
C	Esc	Clears the current calculation.
CE	Del	Clears the displayed number.
Back	Backspace or ←	Deletes the rightmost digit of the displayed number.
MC	Ctrl-L	Clears any value stored in memory.
MR	Ctrl-R	Recalls the value stored in memory. The value remains in memory.
MS	Ctrl-M	Stores the displayed value in memory.
M+	Ctrl-P	Adds the displayed value to any value already in memory.
+/−	F9	Changes the sign of the displayed number.
.	. or ,	Inserts a decimal point in the displayed number.
+	+	Adds.
−	−	Subtracts.
*	*	Multiplies.
/	/	Divides.
sqrt	@	Calculates the square root of the displayed value.
%	%	Calculates percentages.
1/x	r	Calculates the reciprocal of the displayed number. Shows the result of dividing the displayed number into 1.
=	= or ↵	Displays the results of an operation on the previous two numbers.

TABLE 24.1:

Keyboard Equivalents for the Nonnumeric Buttons on the Standard Calculator

Let's practice calculating the total sales price on several items, including a 6% tax.

1. Double-click on the Calculator icon to display the calculator.

2. If necessary, turn on your numeric keypad by pressing Num Lock. If your keyboard has indicators, the Num Lock indicator will light.

3. Enter **36.60**. You can either click on each of the keys that make up the number or type them using the numeric keypad. Remember, if nothing appears on-screen when you are using the keyboard, then press Num Lock once.

4. Select + or press the + key.

5. Enter **76.45**, then select = or press ↵. The sum of the two numbers (113.05) appears in the display box.

6. Select MS or press Ctrl-M. This stores the value in the display box in memory. A letter M appears under the display box, indicating that the value is stored.

7. Select * or press the * key for multiplication.

8. Enter **6**, then select %. This multiplies the displayed value by 6 percent, the percentage of sales tax in this example.

9. Select M+ or press Ctrl-P to add the sales tax to the value stored in memory.

10. Select MR or press Ctrl-R. The total figure stored in memory now appears in the display box (119.833).

11. Select C or press Esc to clear the calculated result. If you select CE, or press Del, only the display will be cleared and the total figure will remain in memory.

12. Select MC or press Ctrl-L. This erases the figure stored in the calculator's memory. The letter M disappears under the display box.

As you can see, the Standard calculator works in the same way as any calculator that you might have on your desk.

COPYING RESULTS TO AN APPLICATION

Occasionally, you might want the results of a calculation to appear in a document or some other application. For instance, if you are typing an order, you might switch to the calculator to compute the sales tax, and then want to transfer the figure to the document from the calculator's display box.

To do this, after calculating the result, select Edit and then select Copy, or press Ctrl-C. The displayed result will be moved to a special application called the Clipboard. Switch to the document window and then select Edit Paste from its Menu bar to paste the result.

In lesson 33 you will learn more about the Clipboard, a program that allows you to move text and graphics among different application programs.

The Scientific Calculator

The Scientific calculator, shown in Figure 24.2, performs more complex mathematical operations than the Standard calculator. Change to the Scientific calculator by selecting View in the Standard calculator's menu, and then select Scientific. Any figures showing in the display, or stored in memory, will not be lost when changing views.

If you are unfamiliar with scientific calculators, the number of buttons may seem intimidating. However, if you look closely at the Scientific calculator you'll see that the buttons near the middle are the same as those used in the Standard calculator, and they operate the same way. The C, CE, and Back buttons are above and to the left. The buttons labelled from A through F on the bottom right are used to perform hexadecimal calculations.

Table 24.2 explains the function of the remaining buttons and gives their keyboard equivalents.

SELECTING AND CONVERTING BASES

Just below the Scientific calculator's display box there are two sets of radio buttons. Use the set on the left to change the number base of your entries—from the default decimal base to the hexadecimal (base 16), the octal (base 8), and the binary (base 2). When you select Hex, the keys in the bottom row labelled A through F become activated.

If you want to convert a number to another base, enter the number and then select the desired base. For example, if you enter 58 in the default decimal base and then select Hex, the display will change to 3A, the number 58's equivalent in the hexadecimal numbering system.

SETTING THE UNIT OF ANGLE

To the right of the base options there are radio buttons for changing the unit of measurements used for angles. By default, the Scientific calculator uses degrees but you can also select radians (Rad) and gradients (Grad) as well.

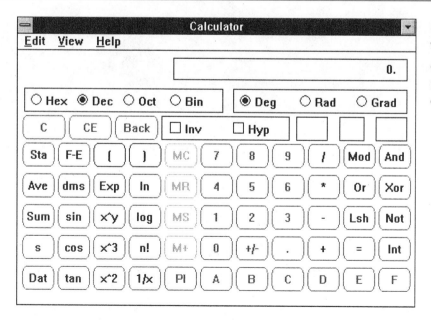

FIGURE 24.2:

The Scientific calculator performs complex computations.

BUTTON	KEYSTROKE	FUNCTION
Hex	F5	Converts to the hexadecimal number system.
Dec	F6	Converts to the decimal number system.
Oct	F7	Converts to the octal number system.
Bin	F8	Converts to the binary number system.
Deg	F2	Degrees as the unit of measure (Decimal mode).
Rad	F3	Radians as the unit of measure (Decimal mode).
Grad	F4	Gradients as the unit of measure (Decimal mode).
Dword	F2	Displays the 32-bit representation of the current number (when not in Decimal mode).
Word	F3	Displays the lower 16 bits of the current number (when not in Decimal mode).
Byte	F4	Displays the lower 8 bits of the current number (when not in Decimal mode).
Inv	i	Toggles the inverse function for Ave, cos, ln, log, PI, s, sin, Sum, tan, x^2, x^3, and x^y.
Hyp	h	Toggles the hyperbolic sine, cosine, and tangent.
Sta	Ctrl-S	Displays the Statistics Box and activates the Ave, Sum, s, and Dat buttons.
Ave	Ctrl-A	Calculates the mean of the values in the Statistics Box.
Sum	Ctrl-T	Calculates the sum of the values in the Statistics Box.
s	Ctrl-D	Calculates the standard deviation of the values in the Statistics Box.
Dat	Ins	Inserts the displayed number into the Statistics Box.
F-E	v	Toggles scientific notation on and off (Decimal mode only).
dms	m	Converts the displayed value to degree-minute-second format.
sin	s	Calculates the sine of the displayed value.
cos	o	Calculates the cosine of the displayed value.

TABLE 24.2:

Scientific Calculator Buttons and Their Keyboard Equivalents

BUTTON	KEYSTROKE	FUNCTION
tan	t	Calculates the tangent of the displayed value.
(	(	Starts a precedence group.
)	)	Closes the precedence group.
Exp	x	Allows the input of scientific-notation numbers.
x^y	y	Computes x (the displayed value) to the y power.
x^2	@	Squares the displayed value.
x^3	#	Cubes the displayed value.
ln	n	Computes the natural logarithm.
log	l	Computes the base 10 logarithm.
n!	!	Computes the factorial of the displayed number.
PI	p	Displays the value of pi as 3.14159265359
Mod	%	Displays the modula, or the remainder of x/y.
Or			Performs a bitwise OR.
Lsh	<	Performs a bitwise shift left.
And	&	Performs a bitwise AND.
Xor	^	Performs a bitwise exclusive OR.
Not	+	Calculates an inverse, a bitwise NOT.
Int	;	Displays the integer portion of a decimal value.

**TABLE 24.2:
(continued)**

Scientific Calculator
Buttons and Their
Keyboard Equivalents

When you select a different base than decimal, these options change to Dword (32-bit), Word (16-bit), and Byte (lowest, 8-bit). Use these options to select the number of bits to display results in the display box.

PERFORMING STATISTICS

The Statistics function allows you to enter a series of numbers and then to calculate the total, average, or standard deviation with the touch of a key. As an example, let's calculate all three statistics on a series of numbers.

1. Select Sta, or press Ctrl-S. The Statistics Box appears, as shown in Figure 24.3.

2. Select RET, or press ↵. Selecting RET returns you to the Scientific calculator while leaving on the statistics function. The other options in the box are explained in Table 24.3.

3. Enter 96, then select Dat or press Ins to add it to the Statistics Box.

4. Enter 86, then select Dat, or press Ins.

5. Enter 95, then select Dat, or press Ins.

6. Select Ave, or press Ctrl-A. The average (92.33333333333) is displayed.

7. Select Sum, or press Ctrl-T to display the sum (277) of the numbers.

8. Select s, or press Ctrl-D to calculate the standard deviation (5.507570547286).

9. Select Sta again. The Statistics Box appears with the three values listed. The notation n=3 at the bottom of the window indicates that three values are being used.

10. Select CAD, or press Alt-A to delete the numbers from the Statistics Box.

11. Close the Statistics Box, then close the Scientific calculator.

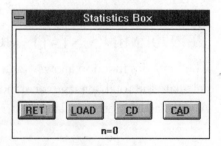

FIGURE 24.3:

The Statistics Box displays the statistical calculation values.

COMMAND	FUNCTION
RET	Switches to the Main calculator window, retaining any Statistics Box entries.
LOAD	The number selected in the Statistics Box copies to the display box in the Calculator.
CD	Deletes the selected number from the Statistics Box.
CAD	Deletes all of the numbers from the Statistics Box.

TABLE 24.3:

The Statistics Box Command Buttons

When you change views, Windows records the setting in a file named WIN.INI. The next time you run the Calculator, it will begin with the same view as the last time it was used.

FEATURING

**Maintaining an
appointment
calendar**

**Printing
schedules**

▼

Managing Your
Schedule with
Windows Calendar

ou can use the Calendar program to keep track
of your daily appointments and to see your
monthly schedule at a glance. The Calendar
can even be set to sound an alarm to remind
you when an important meeting or event is
scheduled. If you are on a network, you can
use the Calendar to check another user's
schedule, and thus resolve conflicts when setting up meetings.

Many of the procedures that you'll learn in this lesson are the same as those used with Cardfile, Notepad, and other Windows applications. Once you learn the techniques for opening, saving, and printing text in the Calendar program, you will know how to perform the same tasks in other applications. So, even if you are not particularly interested in learning how to use the Calendar, you should review this lesson to learn some fundamental methods for working with other Windows applications.

How to Create a Calendar

To create a calendar you must first start the Calendar application and then enter information about appointments. To start a new calendar, follow these steps:

1. Activate the Calendar by double-clicking on its icon in the Accessories group window.
Windows will display a calendar for the current day, as shown in Figure 25.1. At the bottom of the window there is a three-line area to use as a scratch pad for adding notes or other reminders. Above the daily schedule there is a date bar that

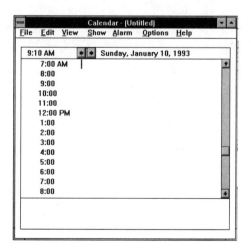

FIGURE 25.1:

The default Calendar window begins at 7 a.m.

shows the current time and date. The right- and left-pointing arrows in the date bar are used to display the schedules for other days.

2. To add an appointment, use the mouse or arrow keys to select the desired time, then type in your appointment. You can use as many as 80 characters. If you type more than 80 characters, Windows will display the message

Text truncated.

The text will not word wrap when it reaches the right edge of the window, but it will scroll toward the right. *Word wrap* means that the cursor automatically moves to the next line when it reaches the right margin and the text moves with it.

3. You can access the scratch pad (note) area at the bottom of the window by clicking on it or by pressing the Tab key. Text will word wrap in the note area so you need to press ↵ only when you have to end a short line or add a blank one. To return to the appointment times area, click on the desired hour or press the Tab key.

To add or review appointments for other days, click on the right- or left-pointing arrows in the date bar. You can also select Today from the Show drop-down menu shown in Figure 25.2. The Today option displays your appointments for the current day. If you select the Date option, a dialog box will appear prompting you to enter the date for which you want to view your appointments. The date must be entered in the MM/DD/YY form.

Show	Alarm	Options
Today		
Previous	Ctrl+PgUp	
Next	Ctrl+PgDn	
Date...	F4	

FIGURE 25.2:

The Show drop-down menu is used for selecting dates.

DELETING TEXT AND APPOINTMENTS

To delete an appointment, you can erase its description from the daily schedule by using the Del or Backspace keys.

The Calendar also provides a way to delete entire appointments from a range of calendar days. From the Edit menu, select Remove to display the Remove dialog box shown in Figure 25.3. Enter the starting and ending dates of the appointments you want to remove, and then select OK.

In Lesson 27, you'll learn how to edit text in the Notepad accessory. You can apply the techniques discussed in Lesson 27 to edit text in the Calendar accessory, as well. For example, when entering a series of regularly scheduled events, such as weekly staff meetings, you can enter the description once and then copy it to the remaining dates. You can move or copy text to another appointment day, or between the schedule and the Notepad areas.

HOW TO SAVE A CALENDAR

After entering appointments into your calendar, you must save the calendar on your hard disk. The procedure for saving it is similar to the way you save documents in other Windows applications.

1. To save a calendar for the first time, select Save or Save As from the File menu to display the Save As dialog box. (See Figure 25.4.) The Save As dialog box is displayed when you are saving a file that has not yet been named. The Save dialog

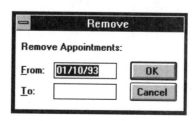

FIGURE 25.3:

The Remove dialog box allows you to remove appointments from the Calendar.

box is identical to the Save As dialog box except for the title. After the file is named, you can use the Save command.

2. Type a meaningful name for your calendar and select OK. All Calendar files take the extension CAL. Windows will add the CAL extension automatically.

If you change a calendar after saving it for the first time, save it again by selecting Save. No dialog box will appear, but the file will be saved again under the same name. Select Save As if you want to change the name or to save it in a different directory or disk.

HOW TO RECALL A CALENDAR

If you want to add or change appointments on an existing calendar you must retrieve it from the disk.

To retrieve a calendar, first select Open from the File menu. You'll see an Open dialog box similar to that shown in Figure 25.4, but it will have a check box for the Read Only option. A list of calendar files will appear in the File Name list box. Select the Read Only check box if you want to display the calendar but not to change it. Double-click on the calendar file name that you want to retrieve, or highlight it and select OK, or press ↵.

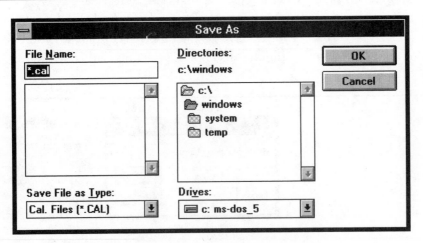

FIGURE 25.4:

The Calendar Save As dialog box displays when you save an unnamed file.

When you retrieve a calendar, if there is a calendar already open in this document window, it will be replaced by the newly retrieved calendar. However, if you make changes to a calendar without saving them, Windows will warn you before you can open another calendar.

To retrieve a calendar and start the application in one step from the File Manager, double-click on a file with the CAL extension. Windows will automatically associate *.CAL files with the Calendar accessory.

Starting a New Calendar

To create a new calendar after you've retrieved an existing one, select New from the File menu. As with the Open option, when exiting the Calendar, you'll be warned if you did not save the current calendar after making changes to it. The New option will clear any current calendar from the document window, just as if you were starting Calendar for the first time.

HOW TO SET AN ALARM

You can set an appointment so that Calendar will sound an alarm to remind you of the event. Move the cursor to the specific appointment and then select Set from the Alarm drop-down menu. An icon of a bell will appear to the left of the appointment time. To remove the bell if you want to cancel the alarm, select Set again.

If you are working with the Calendar at the time that an appointment is set with an alarm, four beeps will sound in the background and a dialog box will appear showing the time and text of the appointment. (See Figure 25.5.) Select OK to return to the Calendar.

Note that the alarm will not sound if the Calendar is closed. However, if you minimize the Calendar, it will keep track of the time in the background while you work with other Windows applications. When the set time arrives, the alarm will sound and the Calendar's icon on the desktop will blink on and off. If the Calendar is not minimized but it is inactive, the window's Title bar and border will blink. Select the icon or the window to display the Alarm Reminder dialog box, and then select OK to clear the alarm.

By default, the alarm sounds exactly on the set time. To customize the alarm, select Controls from the Alarm menu to display the Alarm Controls dialog box shown in Figure 25.6. In the Early Ring text box, enter the number of minutes (from none to 10) before the set time that you want the alarm to sound. To display only the warning box, turn off the Sound check box by clicking on it.

How to Print Appointments

When you are away from your computer, you may need a printed copy of your appointment schedule. To print a copy of your schedule, select Print from the File menu to display the Print dialog box shown in Figure 25.7. Print the current day's schedule by selecting OK, or enter

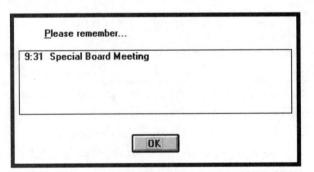

FIGURE 25.5:

The Calendar Alarm Reminder dialog box shows the time and text of appointments.

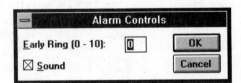

FIGURE 25.6:

The Alarm Controls dialog box allows you to customize when the Alarm will sound.

a starting and ending date in the MM/DD/YY format to print a series of dates.

Like other Windows accessories, the Calendar has many features and useful functions. You can use the Calendar's on-line Help utility to increase your ability to use these features. Spend some time playing with the Options menu and use the Help feature when necessary.

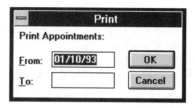

FIGURE 25.7:

The Print dialog box allows you to specify the date of appointment schedules to print.

26 LESSON

FEATURING

**Maintaining a
card file**
Printing cards
**Dialing the
telephone**

▼

Managing Data
with Windows
Cardfile

ardfile is an electronic version of an index card filing system. Although it cannot replace a full-fledged database management program, it can be very useful in keeping track of names, addresses, telephone numbers, and other information that normally you would file on index cards.

Note that many of the techniques for working with Windows Cardfile are the same as those you learned for working with Windows Calendar in Lesson 25.

How to Create a Card File

To create a card file, begin by activating Cardfile and inserting the first card.

1. From the Program Manager Accessories group window, double-click on the Cardfile icon.

Windows will display a blank card in the Cardfile window as shown in Figure 26.1. The bar at the top of the card is called the *Index Line*, which is a line of text, or card title, that Cardfile uses to sort the cards alphabetically.

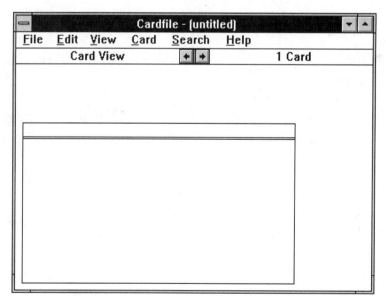

FIGURE 26.1:

A blank card shown in the Cardfile window.

2. Double-click on the Index Line, or select Index from the Edit drop-down menu, or press F6. Windows displays the Index dialog box prompting you for the card title. (See Figure 26.2.)

3. Type the card title into the Index Line text box.

To arrange your cards by alphabetized names, enter the last name first. If you plan to use the card for phone dialing, include the telephone number exactly as it must be dialed, with sections separated by hyphens. For long-distance numbers, include the prefix and area code, as in 1-215-555-1234.

4. Select OK to return to the card.

5. Type the text of the card as you would for an index card. Each card can accept no more than 11 lines of 40 characters each. As you enter text, lines will word wrap automatically. Press ↵ only when you want to end a line or to insert blank lines.

HOW TO ADD CARDS TO A CARD FILE

Once you've entered your first card, you can add other cards by following these steps:

1. Select Add from the drop-down Card menu, shown in Figure 26.3, or press F7. Windows displays the Add dialog box where you enter the title for a new card in the Add text box.

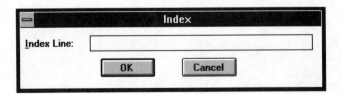

FIGURE 26.2:

The Index dialog box prompts you for a card's title.

2. Type the title for the new card, and then select OK. The first card you entered moves to the back but the card file is not yet saved.

3. Finish typing the remainder of your text for the card.

HOW TO SAVE A CARD FILE

To save your card file for the first time, click on Save or Save As from the File menu, enter a file name and then select OK. The Cardfile program adds the CRD extension automatically. If you later change information in this card file, you must resave it by selecting Save again.

HOW TO RECALL A CARD FILE

To retrieve an existing card file, select Open from the File menu. Enter the title of the file or select it from the list box and then select OK. You can retrieve a card file and start the application in one step in File Manager by double-clicking on a file with the CRD extension. Once the file is open, you can add more cards by selecting Add from the File menu as described above.

You can create a new card file by selecting New from the File menu. As with Open, you will be warned if you did not save the current file after making changes to it.

FIGURE 26.3:

The Card drop-down menu allows you to add or delete cards.

HOW TO CYCLE THROUGH CARDS

Cardfile gives you a number of ways to select cards. To display a specific card, click on the visible portion of the card's Index Line. You can also select Go To from the Search menu or press F4 to display the Go To dialog box shown in Figure 26.4. Enter the beginning part of the card's Index Line, and then select OK.

Cycle through the deck one card at a time by clicking on the left or right scroll arrows in the status bar.

Select List from the View menu to display the Index Line of each card in alphabetical order. (See Figure 26.5.) Click on the Index Line of the desired card, or press the arrow keys, or press PgUp and PgDn to move the selection bar one Index Line at a time. To display the high-lighted card, select Card from the View menu.

PRINTING CARDS

To print a specific card, cycle through the cards until the desired card is displayed, and then select Print from the File menu. To print the entire card file, select Print All from the File menu.

EDITING CARDS

You can delete text on a card using the Del and Backspace keys. The Restore option on the Edit menu cancels any changes you've made to the current card. Once you move to a new card, however, you cannot undo changes made in the previous card. (In Lesson 27 you'll learn more advanced ways of text editing.)

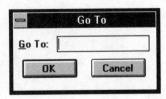

FIGURE 26.4:

Use the Go To feature to locate a specific card quickly.

To change the card title, double-click on the Index Line or press F6. The Index dialog box appears. Change the index information in the text box, and then select OK.

To delete a card, display it or highlight its Index Line in the List view, and then select Delete from the Card menu. Select OK from the dialog box that appears.

To make a copy of a card, select Duplicate from the Card menu.

DIALING THE TELEPHONE

If you entered a telephone number in the Index Line, and you have a modem, Cardfile can dial the phone number for you.

Select the card containing the number you want to dial, and then select Autodial from the Card menu, or press F5. Cardfile will display a dialog box with the phone number in the Number text box, as shown in Figure 26.6. If the Index Line did not contain a phone number, first enter the number in the text box.

The Prefix text box contains the common prefix for dialing out from business telephones. The dash following the 9 causes the process

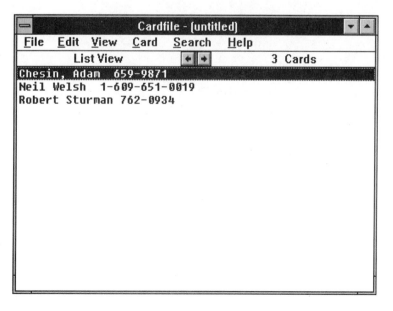

FIGURE 26.5:

Cards shown in List view.

to pause long enough for your telephone system to reach an outside line. To use the prefix, select the Use Prefix check box.

Select OK to dial the line. If your modem is properly connected, the number will be dialed and a dialog box will appear telling you to pick up the telephone.

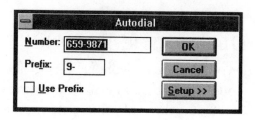

FIGURE 26.6:

The Autodial dialog box displays a phone number to be dialed by the Cardfile.

Making Notes with Windows Notepad

Notepad is Windows equivalent to the tablet or notebook that you might keep on your desk to record messages and reminders. It is like a miniature word processor that you can use to write short notes and memos to others in your office. Notepad differs from a word processor in that it lets you add, delete, or change text in a file but it does not have text formatting abilities. Notepad files are ASCII files, so it is ideal for editing DOS batch files and other text files that do not contain any formatting, such as italic or boldfaced type.

How to Start Notepad

To open Notepad, double-click on its icon in the Accessories group window. Windows displays the blank Notepad window shown in Figure 27.1. Type your document just as you would with a typewriter, pressing ↵ when you reach the end of each line. By default, Notepad will not word wrap text automatically at the right margin. To turn on Word Wrap select Word Wrap from the Edit menu. Any text that you've already entered will automatically word wrap to fit the screen, and the scroll bar along the bottom of the window will disappear. With Word Wrap on, you press ↵ only to end a paragraph or to insert blank lines.

If you make a typing mistake, press the Backspace key to delete characters. You'll learn more advanced ways of text editing and correcting mistake later in this lesson.

HOW TO PRINT NOTEPAD DOCUMENTS

By default, Windows uses one-inch top and bottom margins, and ¾-inch left and right margins. The name of the file will print on the top

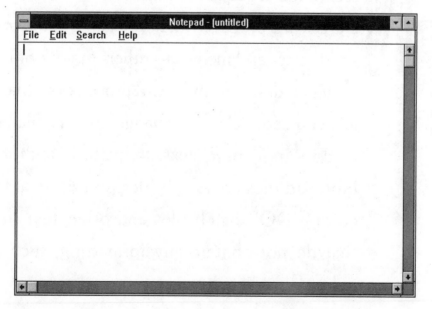

FIGURE 27.1:

The blank Notepad window appears when the Notepad accessory is activated.

of each page, and the page number, preceded by the word Page, will print at the bottom of the page. To customize the page layout, select Page Setup from the File menu to display the dialog box shown in Figure 27.2.

The default header (text that prints on the top of each page) is shown as *&f*. This is a code that tells Windows to print the name of the file. The default footer (text that prints at the bottom of each page) is shown as *Page &p*. This prints the word Page, and the number of the page being printed. Change the headers or footers, as desired, by using these other codes:

CODE	FUNCTION
&d	prints the date
&l	justifies the text on the left
&r	justifies the text on the right
&c	centers the text
&t	prints the time

You can change the margins by entering new values into the appropriate text boxes.

To print the document, select Print from the File menu.

To save your file for the first time, select File and then select Save or Save As, enter a file name, and then select OK. Notepad adds the

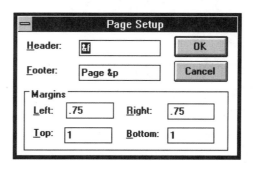

FIGURE 27.2:

The Page Setup dialog box can also be displayed from within Calendar and Cardfile before printing.

TXT extension automatically. If you later change the file, resave it by first selecting Save from the File menu again.

If you are writing a DOS batch file, add the BAT extension, as in AUTOEXEC.BAT.

HOW TO RETRIEVE A DOCUMENT

To retrieve an existing ASCII file, select File and then select Open. Enter the name of the file or select it from the File Name list box, then select OK. By default, only files with the TXT extension are shown in the list box. To display other files, select All Files (*.*) from the List files of Type list box.

You can retrieve a file and start the Notepad application in one step by selecting a file with the TXT extension. If you frequently use Notepad to edit batch or other ASCII files, associate their extensions with the file [notepad.exe].

Notepad will allow you to retrieve a file that contains more than ASCII characters, but non-ASCII characters will appear as nonsense symbols on the screen. If this occurs, *do not* save the file—it may make the file unusable. Instead, select the New option from the File menu, or open another file.

To create a new document file after you've retrieved a file, select New from the File menu. As with Open, you will be warned if you did not save the current file after making changes to it.

Files with the BAT and INI extensions are ASCII text files that can be edited with Notepad. **Caution:** Do not change these files unless you are sure of what you are doing. If you make a mistake, you may not be able to start Windows again.

HOW TO SEARCH FOR TEXT

To find specific text in a document, select Find from the Search menu. The Find dialog box will appear. (See Figure 27.3.) In the Find What text box, enter the text you are searching for, using wildcards if necessary, and then select Find Next.

Notepad will search the document for the text, and highlight it when it is found. The Find dialog box will still be displayed on the screen. Select Find Next to locate the next occurrence of the text or select Cancel to remove the dialog box. If you later want to locate the same text, select Find Next from the Search menu, or press F3. A warning box will appear if the searched-for text is not located.

Other options in the Find dialog box are explained in Table 27.1.

HOW TO KEEP A LOG FILE

A log file records the time you spend on activities. You enter the times you start and end a task to keep track of your efforts, and/or to bill a client for your time.

To create a log file, type **.LOG** at the left margin by itself in the first line of a file. Now, each time you open the file, Notepad will insert the current date and time at the end of the document. Use that entry as the starting time for an activity. When you are done, press F5 to insert the current time. The difference between the two times is the amount of time spent on the activity. Figure 27.4 illustrates a log file used to keep track of telephone calls.

How to Edit Text

Notepad, like most Windows applications, allows you to edit or change text that you've already entered. This includes the ability to move and copy sections of text from one location to another.

The editing process is basically the same with all the Windows applications. You can apply the techniques discussed here to edit text in Calendar, Cardfile, Write, and other programs.

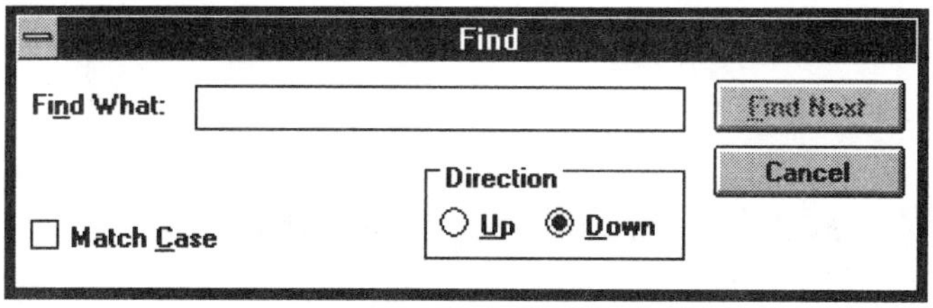

FIGURE 27.3:

The Find dialog box helps you to locate text.

OPTION	OPERATION
Match Case	Locates text only if it matches the same upper- and lower-case of the search phrase. When this option is off, case is ignored.
Up	Searches from the position of the insertion point toward the start of the document.
Down	Searches from the position of the insertion point toward the end of the document.

TABLE 27.1:

Find
Options

Note that after editing a document in any application, you must save it to record the changes onto the hard disk.

THE INSERTION POINT

The *insertion point* is a blinking vertical line that indicates where the next characters you type will appear. When you type, the insertion point will move toward the right. (If Word Wrap is on, the insertion point moves down to the next line when it reaches the right margin.)

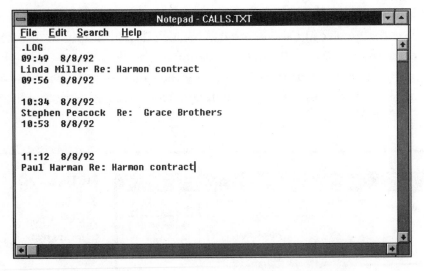

FIGURE 27.4:

A Log file is used to maintain a record of telephone calls.

You can insert and delete characters anywhere by moving the position of the insertion point. With the mouse, position the pointer in the text area. The cursor will change its shape from an arrow into an I-beam. Position the I-beam where you want to place the insertion point and then click the left mouse button.

HOW TO INSERT AND DELETE TEXT

To insert text, move the insertion point to the desired location and begin typing. Existing characters to the right of the insertion point will move over to make room.

To delete text, move the insertion point to the desired location, and then press Del or Backspace. Press Del to erase characters to the right of the insertion point, and press Backspace to erase characters to the left.

HOW TO EDIT LARGE SECTIONS OF TEXT

You also can delete, move, and copy large sections of text using a two-step process. First, you select, or highlight, the text that you want to delete, move, or copy. Then you perform the action.

To select text, move the I-beam to one end of the section you are editing and hold down the left mouse button. Then drag the mouse to the other end of the text and release the mouse button. If you select too much text, do not release the mouse button but drag it back over the highlighted characters. To select the entire document, choose Select All from the Edit menu.

To deselect text, or to remove the highlighting, click the left mouse button.

How to Move and Copy Selected Text

To move or copy a section of text from one location to another, follow these steps:

1. Select the text.

2. To *move* text, select Cut from the Edit menu, or press Ctrl-X. The text will disappear from the document but it will be placed in the Clipboard. It will remain in the Clipboard until you cut other text or until you exit Windows.
To *copy* text, select Copy from the Edit menu, or press Ctrl-C. The text will remain at its original location.

3. Move the insertion point to the new location, and then select Paste from the Edit menu, or press Ctrl-V. To place the same text in as many different locations as desired, repeat step 3 as often as needed.

How to Undo Mistakes

If you delete, insert, or paste text and then change your mind, select Undo from the Edit menu or press Ctrl-Z. If you just deleted text, it will reappear in its original location. Text that was just inserted or pasted will disappear from the document.

How to Delete Selected Text

To delete a large section of text, highlight it and press Del. The deleted text will not be placed in the Clipboard.

Creating Graphics with Windows Paintbrush

Paintbrush is a powerful drawing program for creating free-hand drawings and charts. Even if you are not artistically talented, you can easily create graphics that combine text and basic geometric shapes. And if you are skilled artistically, you can use Paintbrush to create sophisticated illustrations and works of art.

However, many of Paintbrush's capabilities are beyond the scope of this book, so we'll just briefly review its basic functions and tools.

Starting Paintbrush

To start Paintbrush, double-click on its icon in Program Manager's Accessories group. The initial Paintbrush window appears, as shown in Figure 28.1. The functions of the Menu bar options are listed in Table 28.1.

Along the far left side of the window, you will see the *tools* you use to create your drawing. (See Figure 28.2.) The line-size box is below the tools. The line-size box governs the thickness of the lines that you create with the tools. There is a color palette along the bottom of the window for selecting background and foreground colors or patterns.

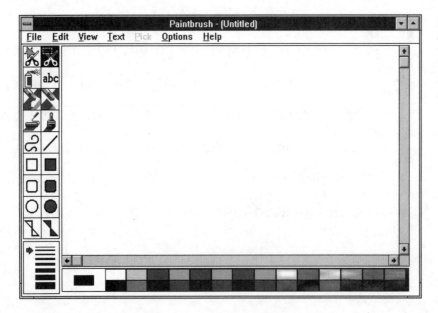

FIGURE 28.1:

The Paintbrush window shows the tools you use to create drawings.

OPTION	OPERATION
File	Open new files, retrieve, save, recall, and print drawings.
Edit	Undo actions, cut, copy, and paste selected areas or files.
View	Zoom in to edit details on a dot-by-dot basis, zoom out to display the entire drawing; toggle to turn on/off the display of the color palette, drawing tools and line sizes; display cursor position dialog box.
Text	Select the font and style of text.
Pick	Flip, rotate, scale, invert, and tilt a selected graphic area.
Options	Change Image size and the shape of the Paintbrush tool, select and edit color palettes.

TABLE 28.1:

Paintbrush Menu Bar Options

HOW TO SAVE A DRAWING

To save your drawing for the first time, select Save or File Save As from the File menu. Enter a file name for the drawing and then select OK. Paintbrush will add the BMP extension automatically. If you later

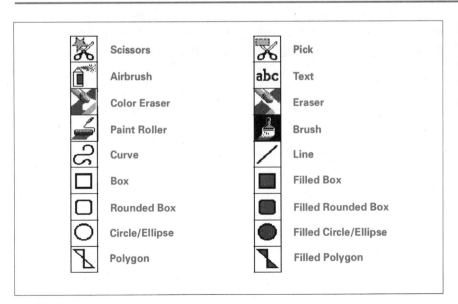

FIGURE 28.2:

These are the tools you use to create your drawings.

Scissors		Pick	
Airbrush		Text	
Color Eraser		Eraser	
Paint Roller		Brush	
Curve		Line	
Box		Filled Box	
Rounded Box		Filled Rounded Box	
Circle/Ellipse		Filled Circle/Ellipse	
Polygon		Filled Polygon	

change the file, you can resave it by selecting Save from the File menu.

You can save your drawing in a different graphic format by selecting a final type from the List Files of Type drop-down list. The possible formats are these:

PCX file	The Paintbrush format. This is a graphic file format that can be used by many other applications, such as word processing and desktop publishing software.
Monochrome bitmap	For black and white drawings.
16-Color bitmap	Drawings having 16 or fewer colors.
256-Color bitmap	Drawings having up to 256 colors.
24-Bit bitmap	Drawings having more than 256 colors.

HOW TO RETRIEVE A DRAWING

To retrieve a drawing, select Open from the File menu. Enter the name of the drawing or select it from the File Name list box. Then select OK. By default, only bitmap files with the BMP extension and DIB extension are shown in the list box. To display other drawing files, enter a wildcard with the extension such as *.PCX in the File Name text box, or select a format in the List Files of Type drop-down list. Any drawing (or document) already in the window will be replaced, although Windows will warn you if you make any changes to a file before opening the next file.

To create a new drawing after you've retrieved another, select New from the File menu. As with Open, you'll be warned if you do not save the current file after making changes to it.

Note that you can start the application and retrieve a file in one step in File Manager by double-clicking on a file with the BMP extension.

HOW TO PRINT A DRAWING

To print a drawing, select Print from the File menu. Paintbrush will display the Print dialog box shown in Figure 28.3. Choose the options you want from the dialog box and then select OK.

How to Use the Tools

As stated earlier, the tools you use to draw with are displayed on the left side of the window. Click on the tool you want and then move the pointer into the drawing area.

Note that before you use any of the drawing tools to create lines and/or geometric shapes, you should first select the line size from the line-size box and the color/pattern from the palette at the bottom of the window.

Now let's see how to use each of the tools.

HOW TO SELECT GRAPHICS

In order to move or copy parts of your drawing, and to use the commands in the Pick pull-down menu in the menu bar, you must select the drawing with either the Scissors or the Pick tool. Using the Scissors, you can select any portion of the picture by drawing a line around it. The Pick tool selects rectangular areas only.

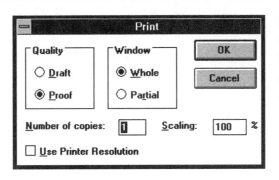

FIGURE 28.3:

The Print dialog box allows you to choose printing options for your drawing.

To use the Scissors, follow these steps:

1. Click on the Scissors tool.

2. Place the pointer near the drawing area that you want to select.

3. Press and hold the mouse button and drag the pointer all around the desired area, then release the mouse button. A dotted line will appear surrounding the area.

To use the Pick tool, follow these steps:

1. Click on the Pick tool.

2. Place the pointer where you want to position one corner of a rectangular selection box, then press and hold the mouse button. This anchors the corner at that position.

3. Drag the pointer to the diagonal corner of the box, then release the mouse button. The box stretches from the anchored position to the location of the pointer.

Once the area has been selected, choose any of the options in the Pick menu. To copy or move the selected area, follow these steps:

1. Place the pointer anywhere within the selected area.

2. To copy the image, press and hold the Ctrl key while dragging.

3. To sweep the image and to create multiple copies, press and hold the Shift key while dragging.

4. To move the image, hold down the left mouse button, and then drag the pointer across the drawing areas.

Figure 28.4 illustrates some of the effects that can be produced by dragging the image and selecting Pick options.

HOW TO USE THE AIRBRUSH

The Airbrush tool simulates the flow of color from a paint sprayer. The line-size option determines the width of the spray. To use the Airbrush tool, follow these steps:

1. Click on the Airbrush tool.

2. Position the pointer in the area of your drawing that you want to paint.

3. Press and hold the left mouse button, then move the pointer over the area that you want to spray paint.

4. Release the mouse button.

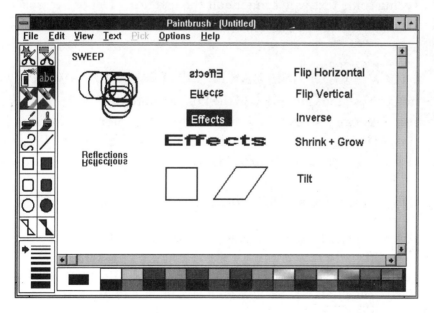

FIGURE 28.4:

Effects created by dragging a selected image and using Pick options.

How to Type Text

The Paintbrush program treats text as if it were a graphic image. You can select, move, and copy text and apply Pick menu options to it, just as you can to any other parts of a drawing. To type text in Paintbrush, follow these steps:

1. Select the font, style, and size you want from the Paintbrush Text menu.

2. Select the Text tool.

3. Place the pointer where you want the text to begin, and then click the left mouse button.

4. Type the text. Make sure to press ↵ when you want to start a new line, text will not word wrap at the right edge of the window.

Note that once you move the pointer and click the mouse after typing some text, you cannot edit the text using Del or Backspace. Instead, you must erase characters using the Eraser tools.

How to Erase Parts of Your Drawing

You can use the Cut option in the Edit menu to delete parts of a drawing. You can also use the Eraser tools. The Color eraser erases only images in the currently selected color pattern. The Regular Eraser tool removes images of all colors. The line-size option determines the size of the eraser.

To use the Eraser tool, follow these steps:

1. Click on the Color eraser or the Eraser tool.

2. Hold down the mouse button and move the Eraser over the area that you want to remove from the drawing.

3. Release the mouse button to stop erasing.

How to Use the Paint Roller

The Paint Roller fills in enclosed shapes with the selected palette color. Note that if the area you select is not totally enclosed, the color will accidentally "spill over" into other sections of your drawing. If this occurs, select Edit and then select Undo. Close off the area using another tool, and then try again.

To use the Paint Roller, follow these steps:

1. Click on the Paint Roller tool.

2. Position the pointer in the area that you want to fill.

3. Click on the mouse button.

How to Draw Freehand Shapes

When you want to draw freehand shapes or just doodle, you use the Brush tool. The line-size option will determine the width of the Brush stroke. To use the Brush tool, follow these steps:

1. Click on the Brush tool.

2. Move the pointer to the area where you want to start drawing.

3. Hold down the mouse button.

4. Drag the pointer to start drawing freehand.

5. Release the mouse button when you are finished drawing.

How to Draw Lines and Geometric Shapes

These Line and Geometric shape tools use a method called *rubber banding*. This means that you set or anchor one end of the shape, and then drag the mouse to form the image. As you move the mouse, the outline of the shape will appear on the screen, so you can adjust or change the shape as long as the mouse button is pressed down. Once you release the mouse button, the shape is set.

How to Draw Curves

To draw curves, follow these steps:

1. Click on the Curve tool.

2. Move the pointer to the area where you want to start drawing.

3. Hold down the left mouse button to anchor one end of the curve.

4. Drag the mouse to draw a line. Release the mouse button when you reach the other endpoint of the curve.

5. Move the pointer to one side of the line, hold down the mouse button, and then drag the pointer in the direction you want the curve to follow.

6. Release the mouse button when the desired curve is formed.

7. If you do not want to form another curve on the same line, click the mouse button on the second endpoint.
   If you want to form another curve, repeat step 5, and then release the mouse button.

How to Draw Lines

To draw lines, follow these steps:

1. Click on the Line tool.

2. Place the mouse pointer where you want the line to start, then press the mouse button to anchor the line at that position.

3. Drag the pointer to the other end of the line. The line stretches from the anchored position to the location of the pointer.

   To draw a straight horizontal or vertical line, hold down the Shift key while you drag the pointer.

4. When the desired line is formed, release the mouse button.

How to Draw Boxes

To draw boxes, follow these steps:

1. Click on one of the Box tools. You can create boxes with square or rounded corners; they can either be empty or filled with a selected color.

2. Place the mouse pointer at one corner of the box to be drawn, then press the mouse button, anchoring the corner at that position.

3. Drag the pointer to the diagonal corner of the box. The box stretches from the anchored position to the location of the pointer. To create a square rather than a rectangle, hold down the Shift key while you drag the pointer.

4. When the desired box is formed, release the mouse button.

How to Draw Circles or Ellipses

To draw circles or ellipses, follow these steps:

1. Click on either the filled or unfilled Circle tool.

2. Place the mouse pointer where you want to anchor one side of the circle, then press the mouse button.

3. Drag the pointer to complete the circle—it will stretch from the anchored position to the location of the pointer.

To create a perfect circle, hold down the Shift key while you drag the pointer.

When the desired circle is formed, release the mouse button.

How to Draw Polygons

To draw polygons, follow these steps:

1. A polygon is a free-form shape created by drawing a series of *connected* lines. Click on the filled or unfilled Polygon tool.

2. Place the mouse pointer where you want to anchor the first side of the polygon, then press and hold the mouse button.

3. Drag the pointer to form the side, and then release the button. The end of this line will be the anchor position for the next line.

4. Click the left mouse button at the end of the next side of the polygon.

5. Repeat step 4 to continue drawing sides for the polygon, then double-click the left mouse button to draw the last line.

Paintbrush drawings can be used with Windows applications and most DOS applications that can import graphic files. Check with the documents supplied with your programs to see which graphic formats they will accept, then save your drawing in that format with Paintbrush. Note that the PCX format is the most popular for DOS applications.

The more you practice with Paintbrush, the better your drawings will become and the more effective their use will be in all your documents and presentations.

29 LESSON

FEATURING

**Writing
and editing
documents**

**Replacing text
automatically**

▼

Word Processing with Windows Write

U nlike Notepad which is designed for small unformatted documents and ASCII files, Write is a full-fledged word processing program. Although it is not as powerful as programs such as Microsoft Word for Windows and WordPerfect for Windows, Write does have the capability to format text (using different fonts and point sizes), adjust spacing, and align paragraphs.

Like Paintbrush, Write is too sophisticated to cover fully in this book. However, in this lesson, you will learn the fundamentals for using Write to prepare documents of all kinds.

How to Type a Document

Write is an excellent tool for letters, memos, and other short documents that do not require multiple columns, footnotes, and other more complex formatting. When you need to create such a document, follow these steps:

1. Double-click on the Write icon in Program Manager's Accessories group window. The Write window will appear as shown in Figure 29.1.

2. Type your document as if you were using a typewriter, except make sure **not** to press ↵ at the end of each line. Instead, let Word Wrap carry the text to the next line. Press ↵ only to end a paragraph or to insert blank lines in the text.

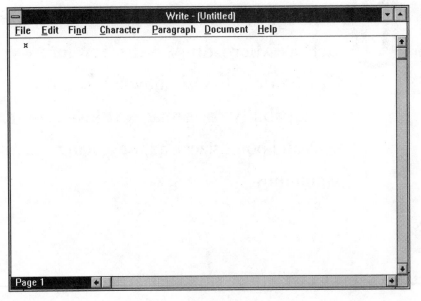

FIGURE 29.1:

The blank Write window is the word processor's startup screen.

3. Edit the document using the techniques discussed in Lesson 27. Use the mouse and scroll bars to position the insertion point.

How to Save a Document

To save your document for the first time, select Save or File Save As from the File menu. Then enter a name and select OK. Write will add the WRI extension automatically.

You can save the document either as an ASCII text file, or as a formatted Microsoft Word for DOS file. Pull down the Save File as Type list and select an option. If the file does not have an extension in the File Name text box, Write will add the DOC extension for the Word files or the TXT extension for the ASCII text files.

The Save As dialog box also includes a Backup check box. When you select this option, Write makes a backup copy of the original file before saving the edited version. Backups of Write files are given the BKP extension, Word and ASCII formatted files are given the BAK extension.

How to Retrieve a Document

To retrieve a document, select Open from the File menu and then enter the name of the file or select it from the File Name list box. Then select OK. By default, only files with the WRI extension are shown in the list box.

To display other files, enter a wildcard with the extension in the File Name text box, or select Word (DOC) or Text files (TXT) in the List Files of Type drop-down list box. When you retrieve a Word or a text file, a dialog box will appear asking if you want to convert the document to Write format. To proceed with file conversion, click on the Convert button.

To create a new document after you've retrieved or typed another, select New from the File menu. As with Open, you will be warned if you did not save the current file after making changes to it.

PRINTING DOCUMENTS

Select Print from the File menu. Then choose the desired options that appear in the Print dialog box, and then select OK. The Print dialog box allows you to print multiple copies of the document, as well as to select specific pages. With some printers, you also can select the print quality (resolution).

HOW TO CHOOSE A FONT STYLE AND SIZE

Use the Character menu, shown in Figure 29.2, to select the type style, font, and size of your characters. Select the options you want, then type the text. To format existing text, highlight the text first and then select the Character menu options.

The Reduce Font and Enlarge Font options increase and decrease the size of your characters to the next available size. To choose a font or a specific point size, select Fonts from the drop-down menu. A dialog box will appear listing all of your printer's fonts and sizes.

Fonts that have the double-T symbol are TrueType fonts. These are scalable fonts supplied by Windows that can be printed in almost any size. You'll learn more about TrueType fonts in Appendix B.

Character	Paragraph
Regular	F5
Bold	Ctrl+B
Italic	Ctrl+I
Underline	Ctrl+U
Superscript	
Subscript	
Reduce Font	
Enlarge Font	
Fonts...	

FIGURE 29.2:

The Character drop-down menu allows you to select type style, font, and size of characters.

HOW TO FORMAT PARAGRAPHS

By default, Write paragraphs are single-spaced and left-justified. This means that the paragraphs are aligned along the left margin with a jagged edge on the right. To change the format, place the insertion point anywhere in the paragraph and pull down the Paragraph menu, shown in Figure 29.3, and then select another alignment or line spacing.

To format text while you type it, select the line spacing and alignment first, then enter the text. For example, to type a headline centered between the margins, select Centered from the Paragraph menu, then enter the headline.

If you want to change the header, footer, margins, tabs, or other formats, use the Document menu. By default, Write uses one-inch top and bottom margins, and ¼-inch left and right margins, with tabs set every ½-inch.

HOW TO FIND AND CHANGE TEXT AUTOMATICALLY

The Find option in the Find menu is almost identical to the Search option that you learned about in Lesson 27. With the Find option, you can locate text anywhere in the document. The Find menu in the Write program also includes the Replace command that helps you to locate and replace text quickly, no matter how many times it is used in the document. For example, if you found that you misspelled the same word several times, you can replace the correct spelling for all occurrences of this word in one step.

Select Replace from the Find menu to display the Replace dialog box shown in Figure 29.4. In the Find What text box, enter the word or phrase that you want to replace. In the Replace With text box, enter the replacement word or phrase. Then, select from the command buttons as explained in Table 29.1.

BUTTON	ACTION
Find Next	Locates and highlights the next occurrence of the text.
Replace	Replaces the highlighted text.
Replace All	Replaces every occurrence of the specified text automatically.
Close	Closes the Replace dialog box and returns to document.

TABLE 29.1:

The Replace Dialog Box Command Buttons

Select Match Case to replace words only if they match the case (uppercase and/or lowercase) of the text in the Find What box. Select Match Whole Word Only to locate and replace just whole words, not characters that are part of longer words or phrases.

FIGURE 29.3:

The Paragraph drop-down menu offers formatting options.

FIGURE 29.4:

The Replace dialog box allows you to replace words in text.

FEATURING

Setting communications protocol

Dialing the phone automatically

Using Your Modem with Windows Terminal

If you do not have a modem, you can skip this lesson and go on to Lesson 31. If you do have one, the information in this lesson will be of great use to you. With a modem you can link your computer to others instantaneously throughout the office, the country, and the world. Terminal is the Windows program that channels your messages to and from the modem. It transfers your keystrokes to the modem and over the telephone lines to other computers, and displays the keystrokes received from distant computers.

The technical details of telecommunications are much too complex for the scope of this book. In this lesson, however, you will learn how to use Terminal with your modem.

How to Start Terminal

You should already know how to turn on your modem and connect it properly to your computer and telephone line. If you plan to communicate with an information service, such as CompuServe or Genie, you must be a registered member and familiar with its log-on procedures.

Make sure that your hardware is set up correctly and switched on, then follow these steps:

1. Double-click on the Terminal icon in Program Manager's Accessories Group window. The Terminal window will appear. (See Figure 30.1.)

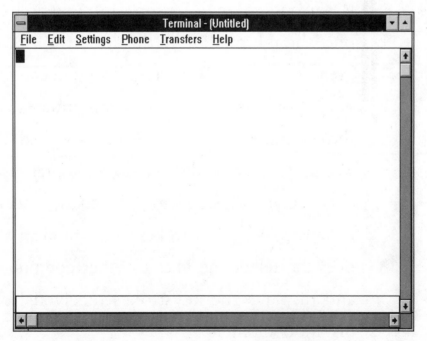

FIGURE 30.1:

The blank Terminal window appears when the Terminal accessory is activated.

If this is the first time you are using Terminal, a dialog box will appear requesting the active serial port. This is the port to which your modem is connected. Select the correct port, then select OK.

2. Check your communications and modem settings.

Before dialing the telephone, you should make sure that your communications settings match those of the computer you want to contact. It is not important that you understand the technical functions of these settings. You just have to be certain that the settings are properly adjusted.

You might have to change the commands that Terminal uses to communicate with your modem. These are the commands that tell Terminal how to dial, answer, and hang-up the phone.

You can try a communication session without changing any of these settings. Certain settings and modem commands have become so popular that they are nearly universal.

Now let's look at how to change Terminal settings and dial the phone.

How to Set the Communications Protocol

Just as two persons must understand the same language in order to communicate, two computers must use the same communications protocol. This includes the communication speed, the number of stop and data bits, and the type of parity being used.

If you want to communicate with an information service, such as Genie or CompuServe, check the manual you received when you registered or call its information line. To communicate with a friend, arrange which settings you will both use, beforehand.

The possible settings include the following:

Data Transmission Speed (Baud Rate)	Ranges from 110 to 19200. The most common are 300, 1200, and 2400. Many information systems can sense your speed automatically and adjust accordingly.
Data Bits	Ranges from 5 to 8; 8 is the most common. This setting controls the number of bits that make up each transmitted data unit.
Stop Bits	Ranges from 1 (the most common) to 1.5, or 2. This setting helps signify when one character ends and another begins.
Parity	Can be odd, even, mark, space, or none which is the most common. Parity is used to detect transmission errors.

To check or change your settings, select Communications from the Settings menu. Terminal will display the Communications dialog box shown in Figure 30.2.

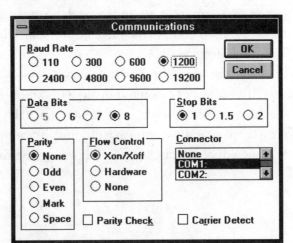

FIGURE 30.2:
The Communications dialog box allows you to check and change your modem communications settings.

Select the options that correspond to the settings you need, and then select OK. If all of the settings except Connector are dimmed, then you have not yet specified the active port. Select a port from the Connector list box to activate the other options.

How to Specify Modem Commands

Modems have a specific command language of their own. In order for Terminal to dial your phone, it must know the codes used by your particular modem. Today, most modems use the Hayes command set, named for the company that popularized auto-dial and auto-answer modems. By default, Terminal is set to understand the Hayes command set and to use a touch-tone phone. If you use a rotary (pulse) phone, or have a modem that is not "Hayes compatible," then you must change the modem commands.

Select Modem Commands from the Settings drop-down menu to display the Modem Commands dialog box shown in Figure 30.3. If you have a Hayes compatible modem but a rotary phone, change the Dial prefix to ATDP. If your modem is not Hayes compatible, select its name from the Modem Defaults list box or refer to the modem's manual and enter the correct codes in the dialog box. When you have completed selecting the options, select OK.

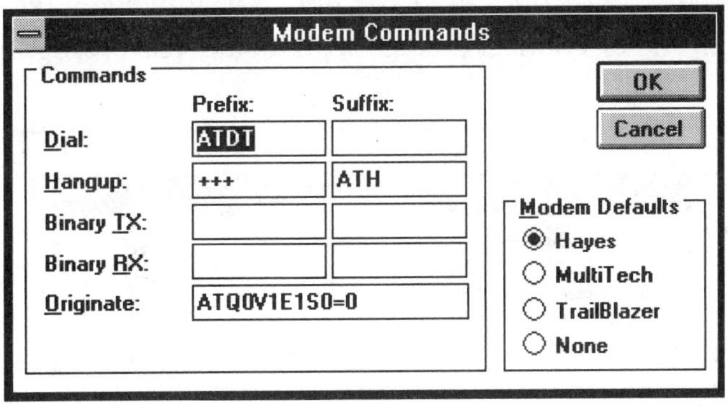

FIGURE 30.3:

The Modem Commands dialog box offers options for your modem selection.

These settings will be the same no matter who you communicate with—they will change only if you purchase a new modem or change phones.

How to Dial a Telephone Number

Once all of the communications and modem settings are correct, you can have Terminal dial the telephone for you. Select Phone Number from the Settings drop-down menu to display the Phone Number dialog box shown in Figure 30.4.

- Now, dial the telephone number you wish.

In the Dial text box, enter the telephone number you want to dial. Enter the number exactly as you would dial it manually, including the number 1 *before* the area code. You can separate the prefix from the number using dashes, although it is not required. If necessary, start the number with 9 to connect to an outside line, or 9, (nine plus a comma) if you must pause before the outside line becomes active. Each comma inserts another two-second delay before the rest of the number is dialed.

When the telephone that was dialed is answered, you'll hear a series of high-pitched tones. These tones inform the modems that both are ready to communicate. By default, if the tones are not received within 30 seconds after the phone is answered, Terminal will end the call and disconnect the phone. If for any reason your system needs more

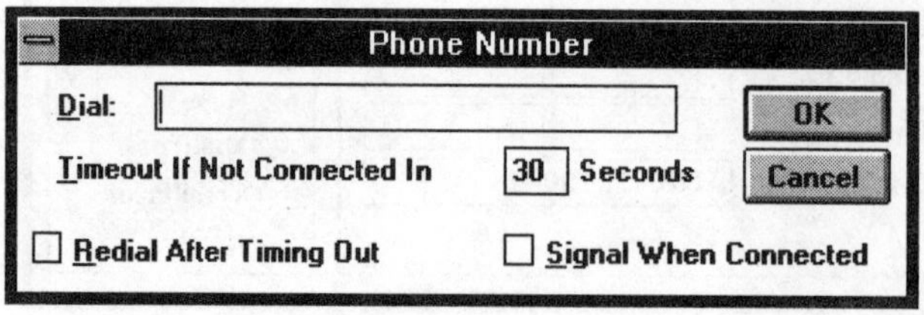

FIGURE 30.4:

The Phone Number dialog box options can dial and redial phone numbers.

time, change the setting in the Timeout If Not Connected In text box from the default 30 to 60 seconds.

To have Terminal redial the same number if the line is busy, or if tones do not sound in the set amount of time, select the Redial After Timing Out check box.

Select the Signal When Connected check box to have Terminal sound an alarm when communications are established.

When you've set the options in the Phone Number dialog box, select OK, and then select Dial from the Phone drop-down menu. Terminal will dial the phone, and display a dialog box with the number and the time remaining. The dialog box will disappear when the connection is made or at time-out.

If you did not enter a telephone number in the Settings text box, selecting Dial from the Phone menu will display the Phone Number dialog box. Enter the number you want to dial and then select OK.

■ Now, log onto the information service, or begin typing.

Saving the Terminal File

To save the settings for future use, select Save As from the File menu. Enter a file name with the TRM extension and then select OK.

Use names that identify the other participant, such as COMPU.TRM or GENIE.TRM. This will allow you to record the phone number and communications settings for each service or person you contact. (Only phone numbers entered using the Phone Number option from the Settings menu will be recorded with the file.)

To retrieve the phone number and settings use the Open command in the File menu.

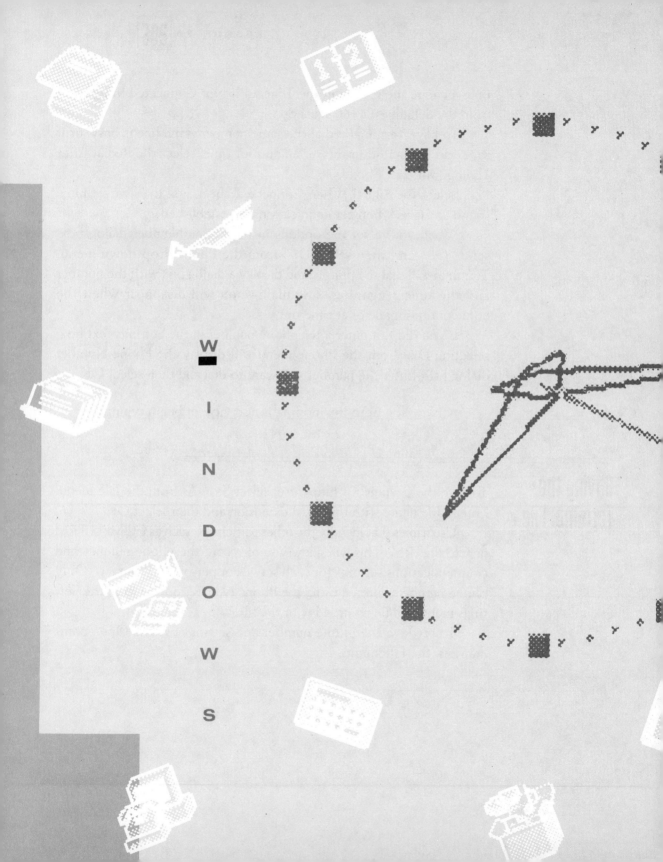

PART 5

Specialty Tasks

As you work with Windows, you may have to perform some special tasks that affect more than a single application. You may need to copy information between diverse applications or to print files generated by a variety of programs. You may even want to create your own groups to manage files and streamline your work. Learning how to perform these special tasks will greatly increase your knowledge of Windows.

31 L E S S O N

Working with Groups

Running a program by clicking on its icon in a group window is certainly easier than having to search for the program by traversing through the directories in File Manager. To customize your system, you can create your own groups of often-used programs. That way, the group icon will appear whenever you start Windows, and its programs will be instantly accessible.

You can also add programs to existing groups. For example, you can add WordPerfect for Windows to the Main group, or often-used utility programs to the Accessories group.

In this lesson, you will learn how to create groups, and how to add and delete programs from groups. You'll also learn how to run a program automatically as soon as you start Windows.

You create a group and add files to it by using the New command in Program Manager's File menu. You also can add files to existing groups by running the Windows Setup program. Setup collects all Windows and DOS applications and places them in a group conveniently called Applications. You may have created this group when you installed Windows in your system.

A group can contain both executable programs and other types of files. By creating your own group, rather than having Windows do it for you, you can include an application and the documents created with it in the same group window. That way, you can start an application and open a document from within the group window.

How to Create a Group

Windows keeps track of a group's contents in a file with the GRP extension. If you look at the Windows directory, for example, you will see files called MAIN.GRP, ACCESSOR.GRP, and GAMES.GRP. When you create your own group, Program Manager establishes a GRP file for it in the Windows directory.

Windows also records the names of your groups in a file called PROGMAN.INI. This file stores the status of the Program Manager window, including its size and position on the desktop, and the names of groups contained within it.

Creating a group is a very simple procedure performed from the Program Manager window. (If you want to create the Applications group, refer to the section *Using Windows Setup* later in this lesson.)

When you want to create a group, follow these steps:

1. Display or open the Program Manager window. It doesn't matter if an existing group window is also displayed.

2. Click on the File menu and select New to display the New Program Object dialog box shown in Figure 31.1. The Program group option creates a new group. The Program Item option adds a program to the current group.

3. Select Program Group, then select OK. You will see the Program Group Properties dialog box shown in Figure 31.2.

4. Type a descriptive name for the group, using no more than 25 characters in the Description text box. That name will appear in the group window's Title bar and below the group icon in Program Manager.

5. In the Group File text box, type a formal group file name of not more than eight characters. Windows will add the GRP extension automatically. Note that if you do not enter a file name, Program Manager will use the first eight characters of the descriptive name.

6. Select OK.

Windows creates the group and displays its empty window within Program Manager. You can now minimize the window to reduce it to an icon.

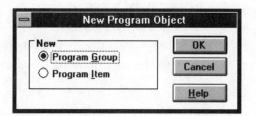

FIGURE 31.1:

Use the New Program Object dialog box to create a group.

THE STARTUP GROUP

During setup, Windows creates a special group called StartUp. A program in the StartUp group will be executed automatically as soon as you start Windows. If you have several programs in the StartUp group, they will be run according to their positions in the window—from left to right, row by row.

You can use the StartUp group to run Windows accessories as pop-up utilities. For example, if you want to display the time during all Windows sessions, add the Clock accessory to the StartUp group. When you start Windows, the clock will automatically appear.

The StartUp group is particularly useful if you use Windows primarily for a single application, such as WordPerfect for Windows or Word for Windows. Insert the program in the StartUp group so that it will run automatically each time you start Windows.

How to Add Items to a Group

As stated earlier, you can add executable programs and document files to a group. A document file must have an extension that is associated with an application, although the application does not have to be contained in the same group. You can then select the document file to run the associated application and open the document in one step.

Adding a file to a group does not remove it from its directory. In fact, the items in a group can come from any directory on the disk.

There are several ways to add programs to a group window. We will discuss two of them: using the mouse and using the Windows Setup program in the Main group. Let's look at these two methods.

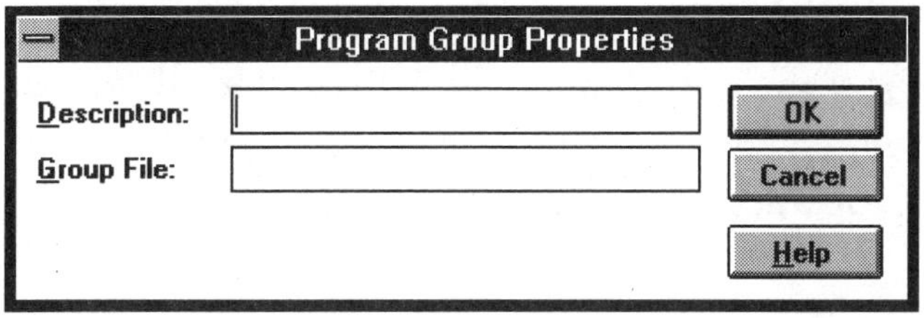

Program Group Properties

Description:

Group File:

OK

Cancel

Help

FIGURE 31.2:

Use the Program Group Properties dialog box to name a new group.

USING THE MOUSE

To add a file (either an application or an associated document), to a group with the mouse, follow these steps:

1. Run File Manager and select the directory containing the file you want to add.

2. Open the task list by pressing Ctrl-Esc or by selecting Switch To from an application window's Control box. Select the Tile option.

Both the File Manager and Program Manager windows will be displayed.

3. Scroll the directory contents list of the directory window so that you can see the name of the file to be added.

4. Scroll the Program Manager window so that you can see the icon of the group to which you are adding the file. You can open the group window, if desired.

5. Highlight the file in File Manager. Note that you can select and add more than one file at a time.

6. Drag the file onto the group icon, or into the open group window, and then release the mouse button. As you drag the file, a black and white file icon moves with the pointer.

An icon of the file will appear in the group window, although it will not be the same icon as appeared in File Manager. If you do not like the placement of the icons, drag them around the window or select Arrange Icons from the Window menu.

There are some options you can add to a group item that will affect how the group item will be executed. If you want to change these options after adding a program, read the section "Changing Item Properties" in this lesson.

USING WINDOWS SETUP

You can use Windows Setup program to add group items in two ways. You can manually specify the file (program item) that you want to add and the group to which you want to add it. Also, you can have Setup search your hard disk looking for Windows and DOS applications, and then add them to the applications group. This saves you the trouble of manually creating the group and moving programs into it.

If you performed an express setup when you installed Windows, the Setup program created the Applications group for you. If you want to add applications that you've installed since then, you can run Setup from the Main group window.

Let's look at both uses of Setup.

Specifying a File and Group

If you want to add only a single file to a group, you can save time by entering its name in a dialog box. Here are the steps to do this:

1. Open the Main group window and then double-click on the Windows Setup icon.

2. Select Set Up Application from the Options menu. The Setup Applications dialog box shown in Figure 31.3 will appear.

FIGURE 31.3:

You can select the way you want to set up an application.

3. Select the Ask you to specify an application radio button. Then select OK. The Setup Applications dialog box takes the form of the dialog box shown in Figure 31.4.

4. Enter the path and filename of the application in the text box. If you are not sure of the filename and path, use the Browse button.

5. By default, the Add to Program Group box is set at Applications. If you select this, Windows will create the group if it does not already exist.
   To select another group, click on the down arrow button to display the drop-down list box, which contains the names of your existing groups. Then select another group.

6. Select OK.

Windows will add the designated file to the group, and then return to Program Manager.

Adding Files Automatically

If you want to add programs to the Applications group, you can have Setup help you. It will scan the hard disk looking for applications just as it did when you first installed Windows. However, Setup will only recognize DOS applications for which it has a Program Information File (PIF). Windows comes with PIF files for most major applications.

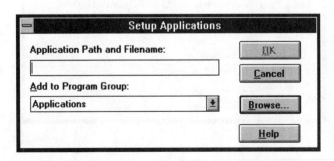

FIGURE 31.4:

The Setup Applications dialog box is for specifying an application and a group.

In addition, many DOS programs come with PIF files for use with Windows. If your DOS programs have PIF files, copy the PIF file to the Windows directory before starting Setup.

Once Setup has identified the programs on your hard disk, you can then select the ones you want to add to a group.

To add programs using Setup, follow these steps:

1. Open the Main group window and double-click on the Windows Setup icon.

2. Select Setup Applications from the Options menu.

3. Select the Search for applications radio button, and then select OK. The Setup Applications dialog box takes the form of the dialog box shown in Figure 31.5.

4. Click on each drive name to highlight all disk drives. Then select Search Now to search all of your disk drives, or select a specific drive or path.

5. If Windows locates a DOS application that it cannot identify, it will display a dialog box asking you to select the application name. (See Appendix A for this dialog box.) Highlight the name of the application in the list box that appears, and then press ↵.

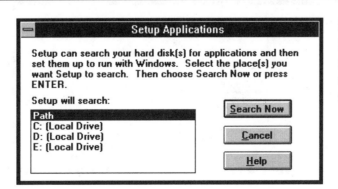

FIGURE 31.5:

Setup allows you to specify the disk or path to scan for applications.

Press Esc if you do not want to install the program.
A dialog box will appear listing the names of the applications in a list box on the left side. (See Figure 31.6.)

6. Select the application you want to add, then select Add (Alt-A).

7. Select OK.

Setup will add the programs to the Applications group, and then return to Windows Setup dialog box.

CHANGING ITEM PROPERTIES

You can customize the appearance of a program item and how it is executed by changing its properties. Open the group window containing the program you want to customize, and then click on the item to select it. Pull down the File menu and select Properties (Alt-⏎) to display the dialog box shown in Figure 31.7.

■ In the Description text box, change the label that appears under the icon and in the program window's Title bar.

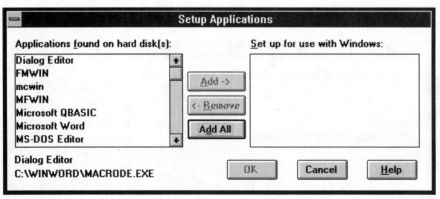

FIGURE 31.6:

Select the applications you want to insert in the group, then select Add.

- In the Command Line text box, confirm the name and path of the application. To open a document as soon as the program is executed, after the application pathname, enter a space followed by the document file's pathname, such as

C:\WINDOWS\WINWORD.EXE C:\DOCS\BUDGET.93

- In the Working Directory text box, specify a directory that you want the application to use as its default. For example, if you are changing the properties for the DOS version of WordPerfect, entering C:\DOCS will cause the contents of C:\DOCS to appear when you select List Files (by pressing F5) in WordPerfect for DOS.

- You can always switch to an inactive application using the Task List or Windows' shortcut keys. In the Shortcut Key text box, enter another shortcut key that you want to use to make this application active if it has been placed in the background. The word None will be replaced as soon as you enter the shortcut keystrokes.

- Select Run Minimized if you want the program to be minimized as soon as it is executed.

- Select Change Icon to see other possible icons for the application. (See Figure 31.8.) Note that some programs will not have alternate icons from which to select.

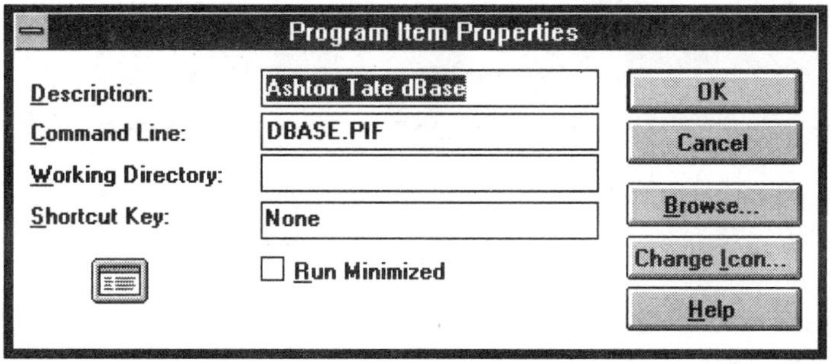

FIGURE 31.7:

You can change the name of the program with the Program Item Properties dialog box.

To add an item to a group and change its properties in one step, first open the group window or select the group icon in Program Manager. Select New in the File menu, then Program Item, and then select OK. The Properties dialog box will appear but without any entries in the text boxes. Complete the text boxes, then select OK to insert the item into the group.

Deleting Items from a Group

Deleting a file from a group does not remove it from your disk, it simply removes the file's icon from the group window.

To delete an item from a group, highlight its icon in the group window, and then press Del, or select Delete from the File menu. Select Yes from the confirmation dialog box that will appear.

To Delete an Entire Group

To delete a group itself, reduce the group window to an icon in Program Manager. Highlight the icon, and then press Del or select Delete from the File menu. Select Yes from the confirmation dialog box that will appear.

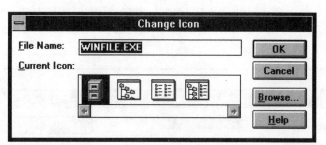

FIGURE 31.8:

Some applications have alternate icons that you can select.

Moving and Copying Group Items

You can easily move or copy a group item to another group. Using the mouse, drag the item's icon onto the other group's icon, or into its open window. To copy an item, hold down the Ctrl key while you drag the icon. To move an item, do **not** press Ctrl while dragging. You can also make a duplicate copy of an item in the same group. Press Ctrl and drag the icon to another location in the same window.

Having an item in two groups, or two copies of the item in the same group, can be useful because each one can have different properties. For example, suppose you have two subdirectories that contain your WordPerfect for Windows documents. Copy the WordPerfect item either to the same or a different group. Highlight one of the items, and then change its properties. Use a different description so you can tell them apart and enter one of the subdirectories into the Working Directory text box.

Highlight the other icon and enter the second subdirectory into its Working Directory text box. Now, you can start the application using either subdirectory as the default by double-clicking the corresponding icon.

Printing Files

Most of the time, you will find it more convenient to print a document from within the application you used to create it. All Windows applications have a Print option in the File menu. Start the application, open the file that you want to print, and then select Print from the File menu. Respond to the dialog box that may appear, and then select OK.

You can also print files directly from the File Manager window, as long as the file has an extension associated with a Windows application.

If you are using a DOS application from within Windows, however, you must use the application to print files. Check the program's manual to see how to print a file.

In this lesson, you will learn how to print files from File Manager and how to use Print Manager, the Windows program that controls the printing process. Print Manager is activated only when you print from a Windows application. When you print from a DOS application, even one running in a window under Enhanced mode, the application's own print function is used.

Printing Document Files

Highlight the document file (that's associated with its application) in the directory contents list in File Manager, and then select Print from the File menu. Windows will display the Print dialog box shown in Figure 32.1. Select OK to start printing.

Windows will transfer the request to the associated application and begin its print procedure. A small dialog box will appear as the print request is transferred to Print Manager. To cancel printing, select Cancel in the dialog box. Print Manager will send the document to the printer as long as it is installed and set up properly.

If you have trouble printing, refer to Appendix B.

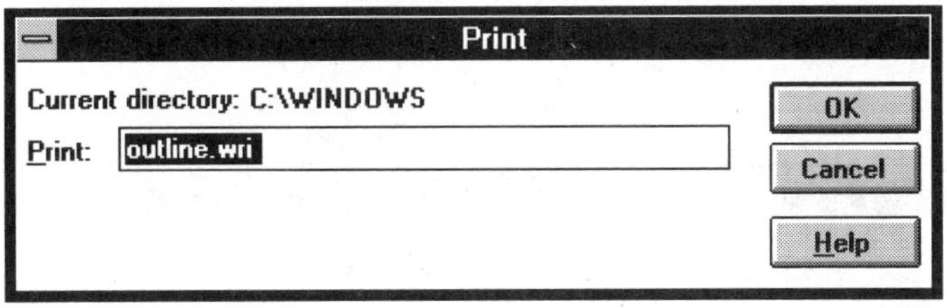

FIGURE 32.1:

The Print dialog box appears when you select Print from the File menu.

PRINTING MULTIPLE FILES

You can select more than one document to print, even documents created with different applications. Windows can hold as many of the file names as possible in the Print text box, but all of the selected files will be printed in the order in which they appear in the directory contents list.

Using Print Manager

Print Manager places Windows print requests in a waiting line, called a *queue*. As long as nothing goes wrong with your printer, your document will be printed when its turn comes up in the queue. However, things do go wrong—ribbons break, toner needs replenishing, you could run out of paper. When such a printer error occurs, Print Manager will stop printing until you correct the problem and tell it to resume printing.

If your printer is set for manual feed and runs out of paper, Print Manager will wait until you insert a sheet of paper and instruct it to begin printing. You have to run Print Manager and give the command to begin printing after you load each sheet of paper.

When you are working with a Windows application and something halts the printing process, a dialog box similar to the one shown in Figure 32.2 will appear.

Correct the problem, and then select Retry. If you are not sure of the problem, select Cancel. The application might continue to send the document to Print Manager, although it is not able to print it. You must correct the problem and then access Print Manager to continue printing.

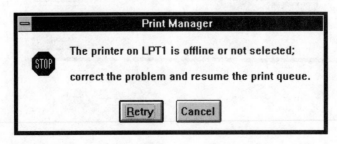

FIGURE 32.2:

The Print Manager dialog box warns you that the job cannot be printed.

You access Print Manager by double-clicking on its icon from the Main window. If you are running a Windows application, such as Word for Windows, you can minimize the application window to an icon so that you can return to it quickly. You can also display the application and Print Manager in their own windows on the screen, and then switch back and forth between the two. This is particularly convenient if you are using a non-laser printer with manually fed paper because you can switch to Print Manager to instruct it to begin printing without having to exit the application.

When Print Manager becomes active, you'll see its icon at the bottom of the desktop. (You won't see it if you are running an application full-screen.) Minimize or restore the application, then double-click on the Print Manager icon. With the keyboard, use the Task List. The Print Manager window is shown in Figure 32.3.

Correct the problem with the printer, then click the Resume button. You can then exit Print Manager and return to your application, or begin another Windows task. With both Print Manager and a Windows application running, you can switch back and forth between the two by pressing Alt-Tab.

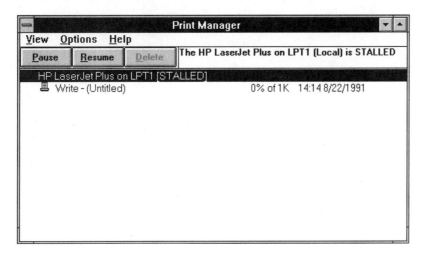

FIGURE 32.3:

The Print Manager window offers options to resume or delete print jobs.

Wait until all of the documents in the queue are printed before you close Print Manager. If you try to close Print Manager while it still has documents to print, you'll see a dialog box with the message

Closing Print Manager will cancel all pending print jobs.

If you don't want to cancel your print jobs, select Cancel.

Remember, *always* save your document before attempting to print it. If the worst occurs and you have to exit Windows before returning to the application, the document will be safely stored on your disk.

BYPASSING PRINT MANAGER

Depending on your hardware, you might find that Print Manager slows down the printing process. You can bypass Print Manager, but then printing cannot take place in the background. You will not be able to use or exit the application until the document has been printed. How to bypass Print Manager and other printer options are discussed in Appendix B.

33 LESSON

Sharing Text and Graphics between Applications

FEATURING

The Clipboard

Sharing text between Windows and DOS applications

Embedding and linking objects

Inserting special characters

▼

The Clipboard is an area in your computer's memory where Windows temporarily stores information that is being shared by different applications. When you select Cut or Copy from the Edit menu of the application you are currently using, the highlighted text or graphic is copied into the Clipboard. When you select Paste from the Edit menu of a Windows application, the contents of the Clipboard are inserted into the active window.

In earlier lessons, you learned how to copy and move parts of a document from one location to another. You can also use the Clipboard to copy or move information from one application to another. In this lesson, you will learn some new techniques for copying information into the Clipboard. You will also learn how to view what is stored in the Clipboard, and some new techniques for pasting text or graphics into other applications.

How to Add Text or Graphics to the Clipboard

In Lesson 27 you learned how to use the Cut and Copy commands to place information in the Clipboard from within a Windows application. Now, let's look at some other techniques for using the Clipboard.

How to Copy the Entire Screen

To copy the contents of an entire screen to the Clipboard, press the Print Screen key, which may be labelled PrtSc on your keyboard. Note that the screen will be copied as a graphic bitmap, not as text. This means that you will not be able to insert the text into a word processing document on a character-by-character basis but rather you will have to insert it like a drawing or other graphic image.

To copy the contents of the active window only, press Alt-PrtSc.

How to Copy Text from a DOS Application

To copy text from a DOS application, the program must be running in a window. First, highlight the text with your mouse, select Edit from the Control menu, and then select Copy.

If you are running the application full-screen, use its own facilities to save portions of a document to a file. Save it in a format that you can merge into the other application. For example, save the file as an ASCII text file if you want to merge it into Write.

Viewing the Contents of the Clipboard

Before pasting the contents of the Clipboard into a window, you may want to make sure that it contains the correct information. Switch to Program Manager, then double-click on the Clipboard Viewer icon in the Main group window. A window will appear showing the current contents of the Clipboard. (See Figure 33.1.)

If you are not ready to paste the information into an application, you can save the Clipboard's contents to a file. In the Clipboard Viewer, select Save As from the File menu, enter a name for the file, and then select OK. Windows adds the CLP extension automatically. When you want to insert the saved Clipboard contents into a program, use the Open command in the File menu in the Clipboard to retrieve the file. Note that you cannot directly import a CLP file into an application—it must be moved via the Clipboard.

You can move, resize, or close the Clipboard window just as any other window. Closing the window does not erase its contents. To erase the Clipboard contents, you must select Delete from the Edit menu.

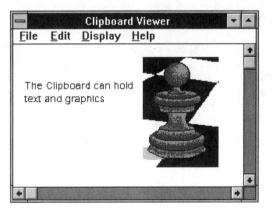

FIGURE 33.1:

The Clipboard Viewer shown with a graphic image.

Pasting Text and Graphics from the Clipboard

If you are using a Windows application, you can insert the contents of the Clipboard into that application by selecting Paste from the Edit menu. If you paste text into Write, Notepad, or any other text-oriented program, the information will appear at the position of the cursor. When you paste graphics into Paintbrush, the portion of the graphic that can be shown in the drawing area will be pasted in a selection box at the top left corner. Move the box where desired, and then click the mouse.

If you are pasting a graphic image into Cardfile, first select Picture from the Edit menu, and then choose Paste.

PASTING TEXT INTO A DOS APPLICATION

When the DOS application is running in a window, pull down the Control menu, and select Edit and then Paste.

When an application is running full-screen, however, the Control menu is not available. Place the insertion point where you want the text to appear, and then press Alt-Esc to minimize the application and return to Windows. Open the program icon's Control menu and then select Paste. (In 386 Enhanced mode, select Edit and then select Paste.) When you restore the application, the text will be inserted in your document.

EMBEDDING AND LINKING OBJECTS THROUGH THE CLIPBOARD

When you paste a graphic image into some Windows applications, the image becomes an *embedded* object. This means that along with storing the image itself, the object stores the information about the original application with which the image was created. This is called the Server application. To edit the image, first select it in the document—Windows will then run the server application automatically. In programs that cannot accept embedded objects, the image is pasted into the application as a static bitmap that has no connection with its Server application. Images captured to the Clipboard using the Print Screen key are always inserted as static bitmaps.

For example, suppose you create a map in Paintbrush, and then copy it to a document in Write. When working in Write, you observe that there is something wrong with your map. If you double-click on the map, Windows will run Paintbrush, and automatically display the map in the Paintbrush window so that you can edit it. When you exit Paintbrush, a dialog box will appear asking if you want to update the map. If you select Yes, the edited version of the map will then replace the one in the Write document.

Linking takes this concept one step further. When you select Paste Link to insert a Paintbrush image into an application, a copy of the image in the Clipboard will be displayed in the document, but it only represents the image. The Paste Link command actually inserts the name of the Paintbrush file that contains the image into the document. If you change the drawing later, and save it again to the same file, the pasted copy will change automatically. Linking ensures that the most recent version of a file is the one that will be printed with the document.

With Cardfile, you can insert a graphic by first selecting Picture from the Edit menu, and then Paste or Paste Link from the Edit menu.

The Edit menus in some applications contain additional options that are shown in Table 33.1.

INSERTING SPECIAL CHARACTERS

You can use the Character Map program in the Accessories Group to insert special characters and symbols into your documents through the Clipboard. To insert a special character follow these steps:

1. In the Accessories group window, double-click on the Character Map icon to display the dialog box shown in Figure 33.2.

OPTIONS	OPERATION
Copy To	Saves the selection to a disk file.
Paste From	Inserts the contents of a disk file.
Links	Allows you to update, cancel, change, or edit a link.
Paste Special	Allows you to paste or link an object, and select a type other than the default.

TABLE 33.1:

Other Edit Options

2. Pull down the Font list box and select the font that contains the character you want to insert. When you select a font, the characters in it will appear in the table in the dialog box. To see an enlarged display of a character, point to it and hold down the mouse button. Drag the mouse to display each character the pointer touches.

3. Double-click on the character you want to insert. The character will appear in the Characters to Copy text box. Repeat this step to select all of the characters you want to copy.

4. Select Copy, then select Close.

5. Open or switch to the document into which you want to insert the characters, then select Paste from the Edit menu.

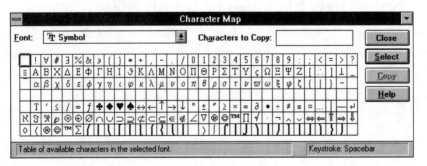

FIGURE 33.2:

The Character Map dialog box allows you to insert special characters and symbols into your documents.

6. If incorrect characters appear, reselect the characters you want and then use the application's Character, Font, or other menu to select the same font you chose in the Character Map dialog box. For example, if you copied characters from the True Type Symbol font, then you must format the characters in the True Type Symbol font in the document to which they are being inserted.

Returning to DOS Temporarily

ou should be able to perform any computer operation from within the Windows environment. However, if you must return to the DOS level, you can do so without exiting Windows. Your Windows applications will remain open, and your documents will stay just as you left them.

How to Access the DOS Prompt

To access the DOS prompt without leaving Windows, double-click on the DOS prompt in the Main group window. If you are running in Standard mode, the screen will clear and you'll see the DOS prompt and the following message

Type EXIT and press ENTER to quit this MS-DOS prompt and return to Windows.
Press ALT-TAB to switch to Windows or another application.

Perform whatever operation you wish to, and then at the DOS prompt, type Exit and press ↵. The Windows screen will appear just as you left it.

If you are running in 386 Enhanced mode, the prompt will include a third option:

Press ALT-ENTER to switch this MS-DOS prompt between a window and full-screen.

Caution: When you are at the DOS prompt from within Windows, do **not** turn off your computer. If you do, you could damage any files or open documents that are being retained by Windows. To quit, return to Windows, close your applications, and then exit Windows normally.

W
I
N
D
O
W
S

PART 6

Customizing Windows

When you customize Windows, you fine-tune it to suit your own personal needs, tastes, and work habits. You can even personalize Windows to make it more pleasing to your eyes, and to make the mouse and keyboard more comfortable for your particular dexterity.

Of course, you may choose not to personalize Windows. Nevertheless, if you do, you may find that it increases your productivity and personal satisfaction in the same way that personalizing an exercise program does. Customizing Windows can create a system that matches your unique requirements.

35 L E S S O N

Setting the Screen Colors

The Control Panel application in the Main group allows you to customize Windows environment settings. With it you can perform the following actions.

- Adjust the screen colors

- Add and delete screen fonts

- Set up the serial ports

- Adjust mouse operation

- Customize the desktop display

- Adjust keyboard response

- Set up and add printers

- Determine the international settings

- Set the date and time

- Determine how Windows handles multiple tasks and allocates resources in 386 Enhanced mode (when running Windows in 386 Enhanced mode)

- Install, remove, or configure device drivers

- Turn off warning beeps

In this lesson, you'll learn how to adjust the screen colors to make the desktop please your personal tastes.

How to Change Screen Colors

If you have a color monitor, Windows assigns default colors to each element of the screen. However, if you find Windows default colors do not please you, you can change the colors and even create your own custom colors.

1. In the Main group window, double-click on the Control Panel icon. Figure 35.1 shows the Control Panel window with icons for each part of Windows that can be customized. Note that the 386 Enhanced option will appear only if you are running in that mode.

2. Double-click on the Color icon. The Color dialog box will open, displaying a sample of the desktop and options for selecting Color Schemes and Color Palettes. (See Figure 35.2.)

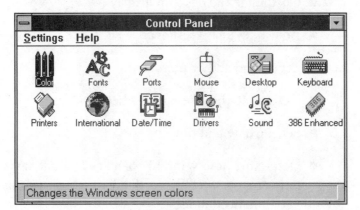

FIGURE 35.1:

The Control Panel window allows you to customize Windows environment settings.

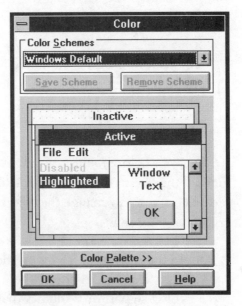

FIGURE 35.2:

The Color dialog box allows you to customize your colors.

The Color Scheme drop-down list box contains several predefined sets of colors. When you select one of the schemes, the sample desktop will change to display its colors.

3. Try each of the alternate schemes. If you find one that you like, select OK to apply it to the desktop and then return to the Control Panel. If you want to create a customized color scheme, continue following these steps from within the Color dialog box.

4. Click on the Color Palette button to expand the Color dialog box as shown in Figure 35.3. (Note that although the figure is printed in black and white, your monitor will display the colors that it is capable of producing.)

5. Use the Screen Element drop-down list box to select a part of the screen that you want to customize, such as the Active Title bar, Active Title bar text, Menu bar, inactive border, and so on.

6. Select a color from the Basic Colors palette.

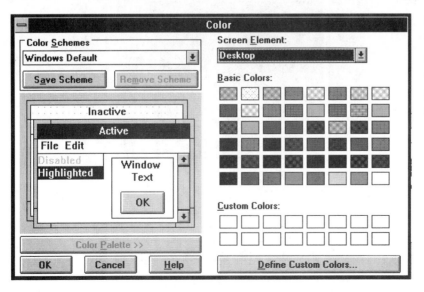

FIGURE 35.3:

The expanded Color dialog box with color palette for selecting screen colors.

If none of the colors appeal to you, click on Define Custom Colors button to display the Custom Color Selector dialog box shown in Figure 35.4. You can define up to 16 custom colors by mixing shades of red, green, and blue.

The large rectangle on the left of the window is called the Color Refiner box. A cross-bar in the Color Refiner box indicates the currently assigned color. Using your mouse, drag the cross-bar over the Color Refiner box until you reach a suitable color. The vertical narrow bar to the right is called the Luminosity bar. With your mouse drag the arrow up or down to adjust the intensity of the color—drag it up to lighten the color, and down to darken it. Changes you make will be displayed in the Color/Solid box. The shade of the color is shown on in the left, the solid color on the right. To pick your solid custom color quickly, double-click the right side of the Color/Solid box.

When you are satisfied with your customized color, select Add Color to insert it into the Custom Colors palette at the bottom of the Color dialog box, or select Close to return to the Color dialog box.

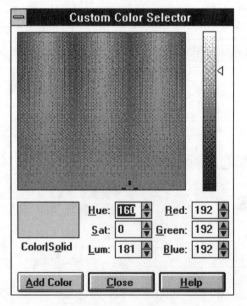

FIGURE 35.4:

The Custom Color Selector dialog box allows you to set solid colors and luminosity.

7. When you have set the color of each of the screen elements, save the scheme. Select Save, enter a name for the scheme, and then select OK.

8. Select OK to apply the color scheme to your screen elements and return to Control Panel.

You can select another color scheme, or customize your own at any time. To modify one of the color schemes that is provided, select it from the drop-down list box, change the colors, and then save it under the same name. You can delete a color scheme by highlighting its name, and then click on the Remove Scheme button.

Controlling the Mouse and Keyboard

Because the mouse and the keyboard are your only ways of communicating with Windows, their performance should be optimized to suit your own taste. By using the Control Panel, you can adjust both to make them more efficient and comfortable for your use.

How to Adjust the Mouse

The Mouse option in Control Panel lets you adjust mouse double-click speed and tracking, as well as allowing you to swap the actions of the left and right buttons. It also allows you to toggle to leave a mouse trail.

To adjust the mouse, follow these steps:

1. From the Main group, double-click on the Control Panel icon.

2. Double-click on the Mouse icon to display the Mouse dialog box shown in Figure 36.1.

3. Scroll the Mouse Tracking Speed scroll box to adjust the mouse speed.

The tracking speed controls how far the mouse pointer moves when you move the mouse. If you have difficulty placing the pointer precisely where you want it to be on the screen, try a slower speed. If your desk space is at a premium, use a faster speed—you will not have to move the mouse as much as a slower speed requires.

4. Scroll the Double Click Speed scroll box to adjust the speed that Windows uses to recognize a double-click.

If you set the speed too high, you might have difficulty getting Windows to recognize a double-click—unless you have very fast

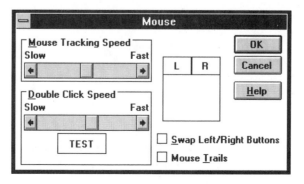

FIGURE 36.1:

The Mouse dialog box allows you to set the Mouse tracking and double-click speeds.

fingers. Test the setting by double-clicking on the Test button. If you're fast enough, the button will toggle between black and white.

5. Reverse the mouse buttons by selecting the Swap Left / Right Buttons check box. If you swap the buttons, you'll have to use the right mouse button where Windows expects you to use the left.

6. If you are using an LCD monitor and have difficulty seeing the mouse pointer, select Mouse Trails. As you move the mouse, several mouse pointers will appear in its path, making it easier to detect the pointer on some screens.

7. Select OK when you have finished your adjustments.

How to Adjust the Keyboard

The Keyboard option in the Control Panel lets you adjust the keyboard's repeat rate. This is the speed that Windows uses to repeat characters when you hold down a key. You can also adjust the delay, which is the amount of time that you have to hold down a key before Windows begins to repeat it.

If you find keys repeating when you do not intend them to, then the delay is too short or the speed is set too high. If the cursor seems sluggish when you hold down an arrow key, then the delay is too long or the speed is set too slow.

To adjust the keyboard speed, follow these steps:

1. From the Main group, double-click on the Control Panel icon.

2. Double-click on the Keyboard icon to display the Keyboard dialog box shown in Figure 36.2.

3. Move the Delay scroll box toward Short or Long to adjust the delay time.

4. Move the Repeat Rate scroll box toward Slow or Fast to decrease or increase the speed.

5. Test the setting by clicking on the Test text box and holding down a character key.

6. Select OK when you are satisfied with the setting.

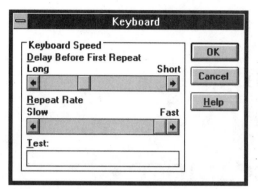

FIGURE 36.2:

The Keyboard dialog box allows you to set the speed of keyboard actions.

37 LESSON

Changing Your Desktop's Appearance

ou can personalize the top of a desk with family pictures, flowers, or small mementoes of people you know and places you have been. You can also personalize your Windows desktop to give it a unique appearance that suits your own personality. In this lesson, you will learn how to change the design used for the desktop and how to control the blinking rate of the cursor.

These options are set using the Desktop option in Control Panel.

How to Change the Desktop Design

The desktop surrounding your open windows is made up of a series of dots. You can personalize the design using either a pattern or a wallpaper. A *pattern* is a small rectangular arrangement of dots, 8 dots wide by 8 dots high, that is repeated to fill the entire desktop. The more dots in the arrangement, the darker the appearance of the desktop will be. A *wallpaper* is a graphic design laid over the screen, similar to the sheets of paper that are pasted onto a billboard.

By default, Windows uses a pattern of dots that gives a solid appearance. You can select from alternate patterns and even design your own. Before changing the appearance of the desktop, however, restore Program Manager so that it does not fill the entire screen. This will enable you to see your changes to the desktop after you make them.

Now follow these steps to see the other available patterns:

1. Double-click on the Control Panel icon in the Main group. Then double-click on the Desktop icon to display the Desktop dialog box shown in Figure 37.1.

2. Select a pattern from the Name drop-down list box. Select None if you want to use a Wallpaper design.

3. Select OK to return to the Control Panel group window and to see how the pattern looks on the screen. Figure 37.2 shows the desktop with the Diamonds pattern.

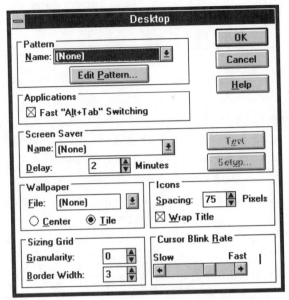

FIGURE 37.1:

The Desktop dialog box allows you to select a design.

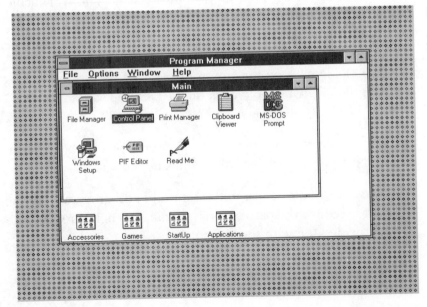

FIGURE 37.2:

A desktop using the Diamonds pattern.

How to Design Your Own Pattern

If you do not find any of the available patterns satisfactory, you can design your own. To do this, follow these steps:

1. In the Desktop dialog box, select None from the Wallpaper File drop-down list box.

2. Select Edit Pattern to display the Desktop-Edit Pattern dialog box shown in Figure 37.3.

3. To edit an existing pattern, select its name in the Name drop-down list box. The dots that make up the pattern appear in the large edit box on the right, a sample of how it will look on the desktop appears in the Sample box on the left. To delete the currently selected pattern, click on the Remove button.
To create a new pattern, enter its name in the Name text box. The Add button will become activated.

4. Use the mouse to change the pattern. In the large box on the right, point to where you want a dot to appear, then click the left mouse button. You can erase a dot in the same way. When you edit an existing pattern, the Change button becomes activated.

5. Once you are satisfied with the pattern, enter a name in the Name text box, and then select Add to add it to Windows. If you are editing an existing pattern, select Change.

6. Select OK to return to the Desktop dialog box, and then select the pattern from the Name drop-down list box.

HOW TO CHANGE THE WALLPAPER

Patterns are suitable only for a desktop design composed of repeated formations of the same series of dots. Each 8 dot by 8 dot block is the same as all the others. Wallpaper, however, permits greater creativity and imagination because it can hold a complete design.

Windows supplies several sample Wallpapers in graphic files with the BMP extension. These are bitmap files that you display, modify, and create using Paintbrush. You can also purchase Wallpaper files, or get them free from bulletin boards and services such as Compuserve and Genie.

Here's how to select and use Wallpaper:

1. Double-click on the Control Panel icon in the Main group, then double-click on the Desktop icon.

2. Select a Wallpaper design from the File drop-down list box.

If you have both a pattern and wallpaper selected, Windows will use the wallpaper for the desktop, and use the pattern as the background for icon names.

3. Select Center or Tile. Center places one copy of the Wallpaper design in the center of the screen. Tile fills the entire desktop with repeated patterns of the Wallpaper.

4. Select OK to return to Control Panel.

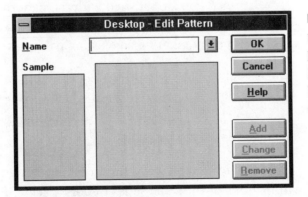

FIGURE 37.3:

Use the Desktop-Edit Pattern dialog box to create your own pattern.

Figure 37.4 shows the desktop with the Cars Wallpaper. To create your own design, use Paintbrush and save your file with the BMP extension.

How to Use the Screen Saver

If you leave your system turned on but unattended for long periods of time, the phosphor coating on the inside of your monitor can become *burned in*. This means that the image displayed on the screen will etch itself into the phosphor and you'll see it as a ghost image no matter what else is being displayed.

When you haven't pressed a key or moved the mouse during a specified period of time, if you have the screen saver turned on, it will automatically black out the monitor, or display a moving pattern. When you return to your system, press any key or click the mouse to return the screen to normal.

You can even password-protect the screen saver. Before the screen saver can be turned off, Windows requests entry of a password that you designate. That way, you can leave your system unattended, secure that

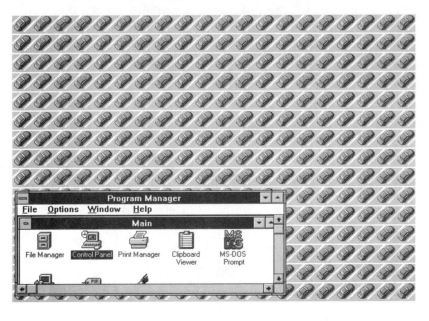

FIGURE 37.4:

A desktop covered with the Cars Wallpaper pattern.

no one can interrupt your work without knowing the password. To use screen saver, follow these steps:

1. Select a screen saver image from the Name drop-down list box. The one called "Blank Screen saver" will simply black out your screen, others will display interesting visual effects.

2. Select a delay time—the amount of time that Windows will wait before starting the screen saver.

3. Select Test to see how the pattern will appear.

4. Select Setup to customize the way the screen saver will appear. The options in the Setup dialog box will vary depending on the screen saver that you select. Figure 37.5 shows the setup dialog box for the Starfield Simulation screen saver.

5. Set the options in the dialog box. To use a password, select Password Protected check box, then click on the Set Password button. You'll see the Change Password dialog box shown in Figure 37.6.

6. In the New Password text box, carefully enter a password of no more than 20 characters. Windows will display asterisks in place of your characters to safeguard your password from prying eyes.

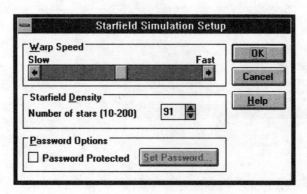

FIGURE 37.5:

Use the Screen Saver Setup dialog box of each screen saver pattern to customize how the screen saver is displayed.

7. In the Retype New Password text box, enter the same password. This protects you from misspelling the password and being unable to access your system once screen saver takes effect.

8. Select OK to return to the Setup dialog box.

9. Select OK to return to the Desktop dialog box, and then select OK to return to Control Panel.

Windows will display the screen saver when there is no keyboard or mouse activity for the set time. Press any key to redisplay the screen. If you set a password, you'll see the dialog box shown in Figure 37.7. Enter the password, then select OK or press ↵.

How to Select Other Desktop Options

The Desktop dialog box contains five other options that you can select to personalize your desktop.

- *Fast "Alt+Tab" Switching* turns off the Alt-Tab key combination for switching between applications.

- *Cursor Blink Rate* determines the speed with which the cursor flashes on and off. Slide the scroll bar toward the fast or slow settings to change the rate.

FIGURE 37.6:

The Change Password dialog box permits you to change your password.

■ *Icon Spacing* determines the distance between icons that Windows places on the desktop. The setting is in pixels (dots). Click on the up or down arrows to change the spacing, or enter a measurement in the text box.
When Wrap Title is selected, the default, long icon names will be divided into two lines.

■ When *Granularity* is set at 0, the default, you can move an icon to any position on the desktop. Any other setting places an invisible grid on the screen. You'll then be able to position an icon so it aligns only on the grid. Set the granularity between 0, no grid, and 49. The value represents a grid pattern with lines set 8 dots apart. A value of 1 sets the grid lines 8 dots apart. A value of 2 sets them 16 dots apart, and so forth.

■ *Border Width* is the width of the border, in dots, that surrounds Windows. Set the width between 1—the thinnest border—and 49—the thickest. The default width is 3 dots.

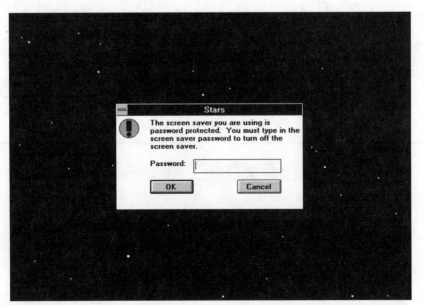

FIGURE 37.7:

You must enter the correct password to return to the normal display from the screen saver.

38 LESSON

Setting the
Date and Time

ach time you save a document file, DOS
records the current date and the time along
with it. You can refer to the date and time to
check which version of a file is the most recent, or to display files in date order in File
Manager. DOS gets the date and time from
your computer's built-in clock, or, if your computer doesn't have a clock, from your entries
to the Date and Time commands at the DOS
prompt.

If your system's clock is not correct, your files will have the wrong date and time. Your clock could be incorrect because of a weak internal battery, a switch to daylight savings time, or some glitch in software or hardware.

How to Set the Date and Time

You can reset the clock at the DOS prompt, using the Date and Time, or through Control Panel.

1. From the Main group window, select Control Panel.

2. Select Date/Time. You'll see the Date & Time dialog box requesting the date and time. (See Figure 38.1).

3. Enter the date and time in the text boxes. With the mouse, you can also click on the up-arrow or down-arrow scroll boxes to increase or decrease the values.

4. Select OK to return to Control Panel.

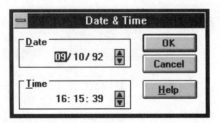

FIGURE 38.1:

The Date & Time dialog box allows you to set the date and time.

Multimedia

I f you have multimedia equipment installed in your computer system, you can access it directly by using the Media Player and Sound Recorder programs in the Accessories group. With these programs you can control MIDI devices, play compact and video disks, and if your computer is equipped with a micro-phone, even record your own music.

To use these programs, however, you must have the equipment correctly installed and you must be familiar with its setup and operation.

Installing a Device Driver

Before using a multimedia device, you must first install a device driver. A device driver is a program that tells Windows how to communicate with your hardware. To install a device driver for your hardware, follow these steps:

1. From the Main group select Control Panel, then select Drivers to see the Drivers dialog box shown in Figure 39.1. The drivers listed in this dialog box were installed into Windows during the Setup process. These drivers are required by Windows and should never be removed.

2. Select Add to see a dialog box of additional drivers supplied with Windows (Figure 39.2).

3. Select the driver suitable for your hardware.

If your hardware is not listed, you will need a driver supplied by the manufacturer of your device. In most cases, the device will have

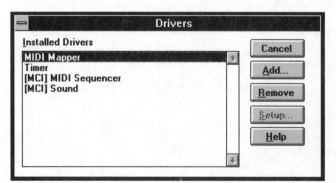

FIGURE 39.1:

The Drivers dialog box accesses other dialog boxes which tell Windows how to communicate with multimedia devices.

come with a disk containing a Windows driver. If it did not, contact the manufacturer and request a driver so you can install the device in Windows. When you have the disk, select Unlisted or Update Driver.

4. Select OK.

A dialog box may appear, asking you to insert one of your original Windows disks, or the disk that was supplied by your device manufacturer, into a floppy disk driver. Insert the disk and press ↵.

For some drivers, an additional dialog box will appear, asking you to select hardware settings or other configuration options. If the dialog box requests a port address or interrupt number, be sure to check your device manual before you select any options. If you enter a port address or interrupt number that conflicts with those needed by other hardware, you may have difficulty starting your computer or running Windows. Select OK when you've completed selecting options.

5. A dialog box will appear, giving you the option to restart Windows. Select Restart Now if you want to use the device immediately, otherwise press ↵ to return to the Control Panel.

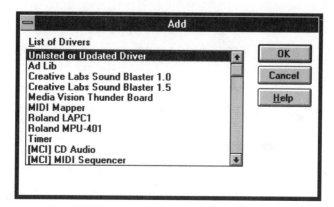

FIGURE 39.2:

The Add dialog box is used for installing additional device drivers.

The other options in the Drivers dialog box are as follows:

- Setup allows you to configure a device driver after it has been installed. The options that are displayed depend on the specific device.

- Remove deletes a device driver from the Windows environment. If you receive an updated driver disk from a manufacturer, remove the original driver before installing the updated version. Never remove the drivers installed by Windows during Setup—they are required by Windows itself.

Controlling Windows Sounds

When you have installed the driver for a sound device, you can assign sound effects to specific Windows events. For example, you can have a certain sound played each time Windows warns you of errors, or whenever you start or exit Windows.

To assign sound effects, follow these steps:

1. From the Main group select Control Panel, then select Sound to see the Sound dialog box shown in Figure 39.3.

2. In the Events list box, select a Windows event to which you want to assign a sound. For example, select Windows Start to play a sound each time you start windows.

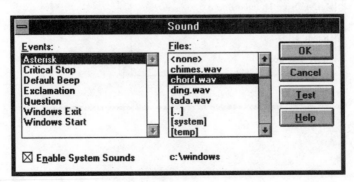

FIGURE 39.3:

The Sound dialog box allows you to select a particular sound.

3. In the Files list box, select a sound effect that you want to play at that event. The sound effects are stored in files with the WAV extension. Select None if you do not want a sound to play at that event. Select Test to hear how the file sounds on your hardware.

4. Repeat steps 2 and 3 to assign sounds to each event.

5. Select OK to return to Control Panel.

To turn off all sound and warning beeps, select Enable System Sounds to remove the X from the check box.

Using Media Player

You use the Media Player accessory to control MIDI devices, and compact and video disk players. You must have a driver installed for the device and it must conform to the Media Control Interface (MCI) standard.

To use your installed device follow these steps:

1. Open the Accessories group and select Media Player to display the window shown in Figure 39.4.

2. Pull down the Device menu and select a device to play.

The names of compound devices are followed by an ellipse (...). A compound device is one that requires you to select a specific file to play. For example, if you have a MIDI Sequencer device, you must select

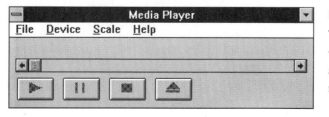

FIGURE 39.4:

The Media Player window gives you access to multimedia menus.

a MIDI file to play. If you select a compound device a dialog box appears, which allows you to select an initial file. Select a file to play, then select OK. To select another file to play later, select Open from the File menu.

Devices without an ellipse (...) are called simple devices. You can play a simple device, such as an audio disk player, just by turning it on and off without having to select a specific file. You use the buttons in the dialog box to control the selected device. From left to right, the buttons are Play, Pause, Stop, and Eject.

The scroll bar indicates the portion of the file being played. Use the Scale menu to display either tracks or time intervals. If set at tracks, the scroll bar indicates the track that is being played, as on an audio disk player. To change tracks or to play a different portion of the device, drag the scroll box, or click on the scroll bar or arrows.

To quit the Media Player, select Exit from the File menu.

Sound Recorder

Sound Recorder operates just like a tape recorder; it lets you play, record, and edit sound files with the WAV extension. To use the Sound Recorder, follow these steps:

1. Open the Accessories group and select Sound Recorder to display the Sound Recorder window shown in Figure 39.5.

FIGURE 39.5:

The Sound Recorder window's buttons permit you to rewind, fast forward, play, stop, and record.

If you do not have a sound device installed, a dialog box will appear with the message

No recording or playback devices are present.

Select OK to close the dialog box. The buttons in the Sound Recorder window are (from left to right) Rewind, Fast Forward, Play, Stop, and Record.

2. To play a sound file, select Open from the File menu, highlight the file you want to play and select OK.

3. Click on the Play button. The Wave box will display a pattern representing the portion of the file being played. Use the scroll bar to move to another position in the sound file. Clicking on the arrows moves you backward or forward 0.1 second.

To record a file, select New from the File menu, then click on the record button. To add your own sounds to an existing file, open the file, then use the scroll bar or forward button to move to the location where you want to insert sounds. Speak or play into the microphone, then click on the Stop button. Save the file using the Save or Save As option on the File menu.

The options in the Edit and Effects menu allow you to perform the following actions:

- Copy the sound file to the Clipboard to be embedded or linked into another application.

- Insert the contents of one sound file into another

- Mix sound files together

- Delete a portion of the sound file

- Increase or decrease the volume

- Change the speed of the file

- Add an echo

- Reverse the sound

To restore a file to its condition since it was last saved, select Revert from the File menu, then select Yes to confirm the deletion of your recent changes.

If you are musically inclined and have the equipment, the Sound Recorder can provide hours of enjoyment for you and others.

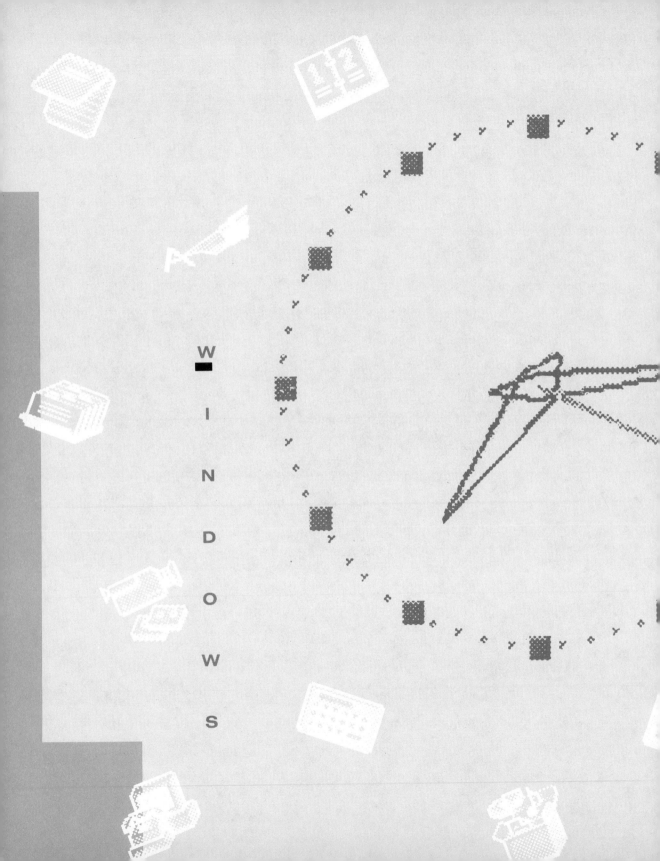

APPENDICES

Installing Windows

In this appendix, you will learn how to make a backup set of your Windows disks for safekeeping, and how to install Windows on your system.

How to Make Backup Copies

You should make an extra set of disks for your own use because disks can wear out or become damaged. An extra set is simply a sensible precaution against losing this valuable program. To make your backup set, you will need all of your Windows disks and an equal number of blank disks of the same size.

Before you begin the backup procedure make sure to protect your Windows disks against accidental erasure. With 5¼-inch disks, place a write-protect tab over the small notch on the edge of each disk. (*Write-protect* tabs are the small rectangular stickers that come packaged with blank disks.) If you have 3½-inch disks, you must protect the side of the disk where the tab is located. You will see a small square hole on both sides of the disk. One hole has a tab that is used to cover the hole. If the hole is covered, the disk is unlocked and files can be erased. You can lock the disk by pushing the tab so that the hole is uncovered. Do *not* lock or write-protect the blank disks onto which you will copy.

Now you are ready to back up your disks. Skim through the following instructions and use the procedure suitable for your type of computer.

BACKUPS FOR TWO IDENTICAL FLOPPY-DISK DRIVES

You received two sets of disks with your Windows package. One set is made up of high-capacity 5¼-inch disks; the other of high-capacity 3½-inch disks.

If your system has two drives of the same size and capacity—that is, two high-capacity 5¼-inch drives or two high-capacity 3½-inch drives—you can make backup copies quickly from drive A to drive B. You should use this procedure even if you have a hard disk and two floppy-disk drives because it is much easier to duplicate disks from floppy disk to floppy disk rather than using the procedure for only one floppy-disk drive.

Your operating system directory contains a program called Disk-copy. This is the program you use to make a duplicate set of Windows disks.

Caution: In the following procedure, *never* place one of your original Windows disks into drive B. If you do, and the disk is not locked, Windows could be destroyed. If you have any problems with the following procedure, consult your operating system manual.

1. Start your computer.

2. Make sure that the DISKCOPY.COM program is on the current directory. If not, open the appropriate subdirectory with the CD\ command, such as CD\DOS.

3. Type **Diskcopy A: B:**, and then press ↵. The screen will display the following message:

> **Insert SOURCE diskette in drive A:**
> **Insert TARGET diskette in drive B:**
> **Press any key to continue…**

4. Place one of your Windows disks into drive A. This should be one of the original disks supplied with Windows. It should be locked or have a write-protect tab on it.

5. Place a blank disk into drive B and then press any key. The copy procedure will run by itself. When it is completed, you will see the following message:

> **Copy another diskette (Y/N)?**

6. Remove the disk from drive B and immediately label it. If you are using 5¼-inch disks, write the name of the disk on the label *before* sticking it on the disk. (You can damage a 5¼-disk by writing directly on it.)

7. Remove the Windows disk from drive A.

8. Press Y, and then repeat this process until all of the Windows disks are copied. Always remember to insert the original Windows disk into drive A and the blank disk into drive B.

It is a good idea to store the original Windows disks in a safe place. Use your copies when you run the Setup program, which is discussed later in this appendix.

BACKUPS FOR ONE FLOPPY-DISK DRIVE

Use this procedure if you are using only one disk drive or two *different* types of disk drives.

During this process, you will be instructed to insert either the source disk or the target disk into drive A. The source disk is the *original* Windows disk that you will be copying. The target disk is the *blank* disk onto which you are copying. *Never* insert the original Windows disk when you are instructed to insert the target disk, or you could destroy your program. To be doubly safe, remember to lock or write-protect your Windows disks.

1. Start your computer.

2. Make sure that the DISKCOPY.COM program is on the current directory. If it is not, open the appropriate subdirectory with the CD\ command, such as CD\DOS.

3. Type **Diskcopy A: A:**, and then press ↵. The screen will display the following message

   Insert SOURCE diskette in drive A:
   Press any key to continue...

4. Place one of your Windows disks into drive A. This means one of the original disks that were supplied with Windows.

5. Press any key. You will see the following message:

   Insert TARGET diskette in drive A:
   Press any key to continue...

6. Remove the Windows disk and insert a blank disk into drive A.

7. Press any key to begin copying.
   You may be prompted several times to switch disks until all of the information on the Windows disk has been copied onto the blank disk. Be certain that the original Windows disk is in the drive only when the screen requests the source diskette. When copying is completed, you will see the following message:

   Copy another diskette (Y/N)?

8. Remove the disks and label the copy immediately. If you are using 5 ¼-inch disks, write the name of the disk on the label *before* sticking it on the disk. (You can damage a 5¼-disk by writing directly on it.)

9. Press Y, and then repeat this process until all of the Windows disks are copied.

   It is a good idea to store the original Windows disks in a safe place. Use your copies for running the Setup program, as described in the next section.

How to Run Windows's Setup Program

Windows's Setup program will copy the appropriate programs onto your hard disk so that you can start using Windows. Setup is very easy to use: Just follow the messages and prompts on-screen and you will not have any difficulties. See Figure A.1.

Before you start, however, look through the materials that came with Windows and find the Hardware Compatibility listing. Locate the name and model number of your computer on this listing and observe whether they have an asterisk next to them. Now, you are ready to start.

1. Start your computer.

2. Insert the Windows disk labeled Setup into drive A.

3. Type **A:**, then press ↵ to change to drive A.

4. Type **Setup**, then press ↵. In a moment, you'll see a screen with these options:

> **To learn how to use Windows Setup before continuing, press F1.**
> **To set up Windows now, press ↵.**
> **To exit Setup without installing Windows, press F3.**

5. Press ↵. You will see the screen shown in Figure A.1.

Most users will be able to select Express Setup so the remainder of the instructions in this section will cover only the process for the Express Setup. However, if your computer had an asterisk beside it in the Hardware Compatibility listing, you should refer to the section "Performing a Custom Setup" at the end of this appendix.

6. Press ↵ to accept Express Setup.

```
Windows Setup
_____

    Windows provides two Setup methods:

    Express Setup (Recommended)
    Express Setup relies on Setup to make decisions,
    so setting up Windows is quick and easy.

       To use Express Setup, press ENTER.


    Custom Setup
    Custom Setup is for experienced computer users who
    want to control how Windows is set up. To use this Setup method,
    you should know how to use a mouse with Windows.

       To use Custom Setup, press C.

    For details about both Setup methods, press F1.



 ENTER=Express Setup   C=Custom Setup   F1=Help   F3=Exit
```

FIGURE A.1:

These installation options are provided for Windows Setup programs.

Windows will check your system for a previous version of Windows. If it finds one, it will display a dialog box that gives you the option to overwrite the earlier version with Windows 3.1. Press ↵ to continue the installation process.

Windows will begin to copy files from the floppy disk in drive A onto your hard disk. During the remainder of this process, you will be asked to insert other Windows disks into drive A. Insert the disk called for, and then press ↵.

7. At one point, a list of Windows-supported printers will appear. Press ↓ or ↑ to select your printer, and then press ↵. A list of ports will appear.

8. Press ↓ to select the port to which your printer is connected, and then press ↵.

After additional files are copied, Windows will build the Program Manager, Accessories, Games, and Startup groups, and then scan the disk for Windows applications and DOS programs with its PIF files.

For most major applications, Windows will be able to identify the name of the program from the file name on the disk. However, in some cases, Windows will display a dialog box asking you to select the application name, as shown in Figure A.2. Press the ↓ key to highlight the

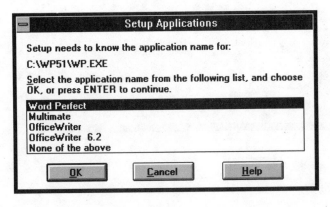

FIGURE A.2:

This dialog box appears when Windows needs help in identifying the correct application.

name of the application, and then press ↵. If you do not want to install the program, press Esc.

Setup will add the programs to the Applications group, and then display a dialog box asking if you want to run a tutorial on using the mouse.

9. Select Skip Tutorial—you will be able to run this tutorial later from within Windows.

A dialog box will appear, reporting that the installation is complete.

10. Press ↵ to restart Windows. If Windows does not start you will have to reboot your computer to load the appropriate files that are necessary to run Windows on your system.

Performing a Custom Setup

If your computer has an asterisk next to it in the Hardware Compatibility listing, you must use the Custom Setup procedure. If you use the Express Setup it could install Windows but it would not operate correctly. In some extreme cases, running Windows after an Express Setup could even erase your system's CMOS information. Custom Setup gives you the opportunity to specify your hardware during the installation procedure so that Windows can install the proper files.

Follow the steps given above but press C to select Custom Setup when you are given the option between it and Express Setup. At one point, you will see a screen similar to Figure A.3. Press ↑ to highlight the Computer option, and then press ↵. A list of computer models will appear. Press ↓ to highlight your model, and then press ↵ to return to the previous screen. Select No Changes, then press ↵ to continue with the installation process.

After additional files are copied to your hard disk, you will see a dialog box that lists specific parts of Windows that you can install. Press ↵ to install all components and complete the installation as described for Express Setup.

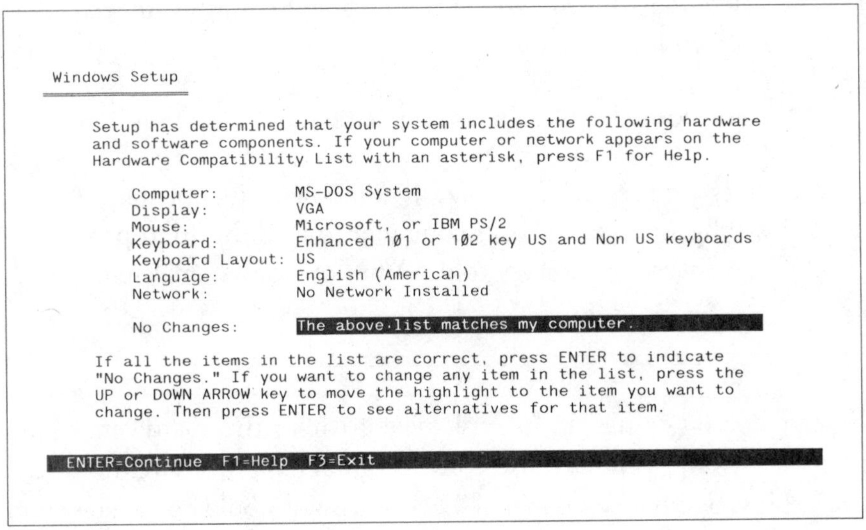

```
 Windows Setup

    Setup has determined that your system includes the following hardware
    and software components. If your computer or network appears on the
    Hardware Compatibility List with an asterisk, press F1 for Help.

       Computer:        MS-DOS System
       Display:         VGA
       Mouse:           Microsoft, or IBM PS/2
       Keyboard:        Enhanced 101 or 102 key US and Non US keyboards
       Keyboard Layout: US
       Language:        English (American)
       Network:         No Network Installed

       No Changes:     The above list matches my computer.

    If all the items in the list are correct, press ENTER to indicate
    "No Changes." If you want to change any item in the list, press the
    UP or DOWN ARROW key to move the highlight to the item you want to
    change. Then press ENTER to see alternatives for that item.

    ENTER=Continue  F1=Help  F3=Exit
```

FIGURE A.3:

During Custom Setup, you can specify your hardware configuration.

Customizing Printing

Because all Windows applications rely on your Windows setup for printing and displaying information, it is important that you properly install any new hardware and software that you may obtain.

In this appendix, you will learn how to install a new printer driver into Windows, and how to configure the Windows environment for additional screen and printer fonts.

How to Install a Printer

When you set up Windows for your computer, as described in Appendix A, you specified the name and model number of your printer. This copied the appropriate printer driver to your hard disk. (A printer driver is a file that tells Windows how to communicate with your printer.)

If you purchase a new printer, you must use the Printers option in Windows Control Panel to add the new printer driver to the Windows environment. You will need the floppy disks that came with Windows to do this, so gather them together before beginning the following procedure:

1. Select Control Panel from the Main group, and then select Printers to display the Printers dialog box that lists the printers that are already installed. (See Figure B.1.)

2. Select Add to display a list box showing the printers supported by Windows.

3. In the List of Printers list box, select the printer that you want to install, and then select the Install command button. You will be prompted to insert one of your original Windows disks in a disk drive. Insert the disk, as directed, and then

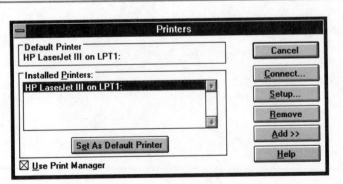

FIGURE B.1:

The Printers dialog box lists the installed printers.

press ↵. The printer will be added to the list of available printers.

If your printer is not listed, you will need a printer driver from the manufacturer. Select Unlisted Printer, then enter the letter of the disk drive containing the printer driver, and then select OK.

The printer's name will appear with the default port, such as the following:

HP LaserJet Plus on LPT1:

If the port shown is correct, and you do not have to configure a serial port, skip to step 7 below.

4. Select Connect. You will see a dialog box showing the available parallel and serial ports.

5. Select the port to which the printer is connected. To configure a serial port, select Settings to display the dialog box shown in Figure B.2. Adjust the protocol options, and then select OK. (You can change these settings later, using the Ports option in Control Panel.)

6. Select OK to return to the Printers dialog box.

The next step is to select printer options.

7. Select Setup. A dialog box will appear showing the available options for your printer. Figure B.3 shows the dialog box for

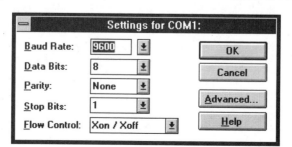

FIGURE B.2:

The Settings for COM1: dialog box is for setting the serial protocol.

setting up a LaserJet III printer. Note that your own printer's dialog box may contain different options.

8. Choose your options from this menu, and then select OK. The Fonts option will be discussed later in this appendix.

If you find that you want to use a different paper size or font cartridge, or to change any of the printer settings, follow the previous steps to display the Setup dialog box. Then make your changes, and select OK.

HOW TO DESIGNATE THE DEFAULT PRINTER

You can have several printers installed in Windows and even assign them to the same port. For example, you might use a wide-carriage dot matrix printer for spreadsheets, and a laser printer for word processing documents and graphics. Both printers can be assigned to LPT1 and connected through an A-B switch.

However, because you can use only one printer on a port at a time, you must designate one printer as the default. Windows will use the default printer for all print jobs until instructed to use another.

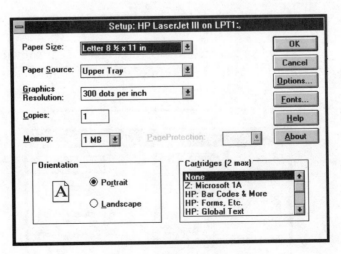

FIGURE B.3:

Setup options that are available for LaserJet printers.

To designate the default printer, highlight its name in the Printers dialog box and select Set as the Default Printer.

If you decide later to use a different printer as the default, select it as just described. However, you can also change printers and printer options temporarily through most Windows applications. The File menu and Print dialog boxes in many applications include the option Printer Setup, or sometimes just Setup. If you select this option, a dialog box appears that allows you to choose another printer from your list or to change some of the options available in the Setup dialog box. Make your changes, and then select OK.

These new settings remain in effect as long as you remain in the application. They do not affect the settings in other applications, and they return to the default values when you exit the program.

Adding Screen and Printer Fonts

There are two types of fonts—screen fonts and printer fonts. A screen font controls the display of characters on your monitor, such as the typeface, size, and style. A printer font contains the data that is transmitted to your printer to produce the characters on the printed page. In an ideal situation, you will have a matching screen font for each printer font, so the document on your screen will appear just as it will when it is printed.

Windows comes with several different types of fonts. In some cases, the font serves as both the screen and printer font—Windows obtains the information it needs for both from the same font file. These fonts don't take up much disk space but when printed they do produce poorer quality characters. All of these fonts use the FON extension.

In some other cases, the screen font and the printer font are stored in separate files. For example, Windows comes with a series of TrueType fonts—Arial, Courier New, Times New Roman, Symbol, and Wingding—a font of graphic characters. A TrueType font is scalable, that is, it can be produced on your screen and by the printer in almost any size that you select. The screen font files use the FON extension, the printer font files use the TTF extension.

You can purchase additional fonts from a number of sources. All files with the FON extension are installed as explained here. You must install printer fonts, such as softfonts used by laser printers, with the Printers option in the Control Panel, as explained later in this appendix. However, if the softfont comes with its own FON screen font file, you still must install the FON font separately.

You can also purchase scalable fonts from other manufacturers, such as Bitstream, Adobe, Atech, and Casady and Greene. These come with their own programs that will modify the Windows printer drivers to install both printer and screen fonts. If you have such a package, follow the directions supplied with it.

HOW TO ADD SCREEN FONTS

When you want to add a screen font to Windows, copy the file to the Windows System subdirectory. This is where Windows stores its own screen and printer fonts. Then follow these steps:

1. Select Control Panel from the Main group, and then select Fonts. You will see the dialog box displayed in Figure B.4. The fonts already installed in Windows are shown in the list box. If you highlight a font, a sample of it will appear in the Sample box at the bottom of the dialog box. The notation (VGA res) indicates poorer quality fonts used to display and print characters of any size. Fonts marked as (TrueType) are higher quality TrueType fonts. The other fonts list the specific sizes that can be displayed and printed.

2. Select Add to display the dialog box shown in Figure B.5.

3. Under the Directories option, select the System subdirectory. A list of FON and TTF files will be displayed in the List of Fonts box.

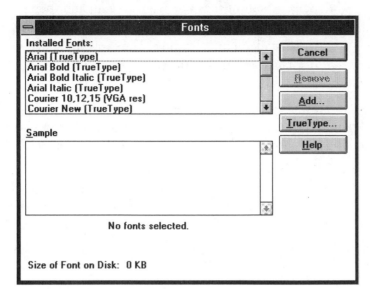

FIGURE B.4:

The Fonts dialog box allows you to choose your fonts.

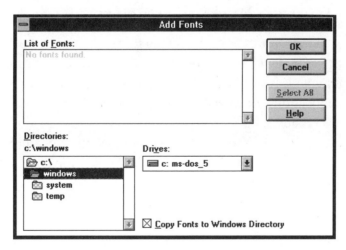

FIGURE B.5:

The Add Fonts dialog box allows you to select a subdirectory and to add fonts.

4. Select the font files you want to add, and then select OK. The Fonts dialog box will reappear with the fonts added to the Installed Fonts list box. The last font added will be displayed in the Sample box.

To control how TrueType fonts are used in your applications, select TrueType in the Fonts dialog box. Windows will display the dialog box shown in Figure B.6. Turning off the Enable TrueType option causes the TrueType fonts to become unavailable to Windows applications. Selecting Show Only TrueType Fonts in Applications temporarily excludes all other types of fonts from Windows applications. Select this only if you plan to use TrueType exclusively.

5. Click on OK to return to the Fonts dialog box.

6. Select Close to return to the Control Panel.

How to Remove a Font

Windows stores all of the screen fonts in memory so it can display characters as quickly as possible. If you plan not to use a font, you can remove it from the system and make more memory available for your applications. Removing a font does not delete it from your disk, so you always add it back at a later time.

Caution: You should never remove the MS San Serif (Helv) font. Windows uses this font to display text in Title and Menu bars, menus, and dialog boxes.

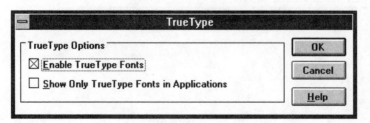

FIGURE B.6:

The TrueType dialog box controls how your application uses TrueType font.

To remove a font, select Font from the Control Panel. Highlight the font that you want to delete and then select Remove. A dialog box will appear asking you to confirm the deletion. Select Yes to delete the font, or No to cancel the operation.

Adding Printer Fonts

If you purchase a scalable font package, such as Adobe's ATM or Bitstream's Facelift, install the fonts by following the manufacturer's instructions. However, if you have or purchase your own downloadable softfonts, you must add them to the Windows printer driver yourself. Insert the disk containing the fonts in drive A, or copy them to a directory on your hard disk. Then follow these steps:

1. Select Control Panel from the Main group, and then select Printers.

2. Highlight the printer in the list box, and then select Setup.

3. Select Fonts to display a dialog box as shown in Figure B.7. Softfonts that are already installed will be shown in the list box on the left.

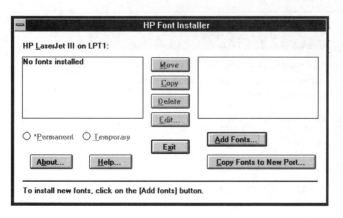

FIGURE B.7:

HP Font Installer dialog box for installing softfonts into Windows.

4. Select Add Fonts to display a dialog box requesting the drive containing the softfonts.

5. Type the drive or directory where the softfonts are located, and then select OK. Windows will list all of the softfonts it finds in the right list box. The Move button will become an Add button.

6. Highlight the fonts you want to install and then select Add.

7. You will be prompted to enter the directory on which to store the fonts. Select OK to accept the default directory, or enter a path and then select OK.

As each font is copied to the designated directory, its name will appear in the left list box. If necessary, Windows will create a matching FON screen font file and a PFM file. Printer Font Matrics (PFM) files contain the data Windows needs to space text properly on the page.

If you want to remove a font later, highlight its name in the left list box and select Delete. The font will not be deleted from the disk, just from the list of those available to Windows.

If Windows doesn't recognize a font that you are adding, it will display a dialog box similar to the one shown in Figure B.8. In the Name

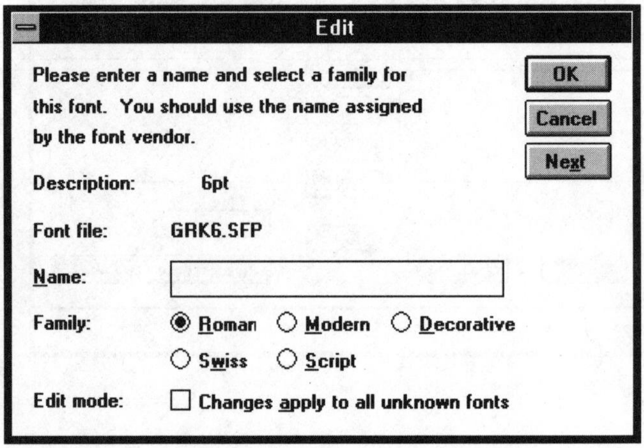

FIGURE B.8:

You must complete the Edit dialog box for fonts that Windows does not recognize.

text box, enter the font name that you want to appear on the Font menus of your applications. Then, select a general family that Windows will use when selecting a screen font for the softfont. If you are installing a series of fonts in the same family, such as Greek fonts in a variety of sizes, select Changes apply to all unknown fonts, so that this dialog box will not appear for each font. Select OK to return to the Font Installer dialog box.

8. Select Close Drive, and the font names will disappear from the right box.

Now, you must give the fonts a downloadable status by designating each either as permanent or temporary. Windows will download temporary fonts when they are called for in a document, but it assumes all permanent fonts have already been downloaded.

9. Highlight the fonts that you want to make permanent, and then select Permanent. If this is the first font you are changing to permanent, you will see a dialog box asking you to confirm your choice. Select OK.

10. Select Exit.

11. If you marked any fonts as permanent, selecting Exit will display the Download options dialog box asking you if you want to download the fonts immediately. Select Download Now if you want to use the fonts. If you select Download on Startup, Windows will modify your AUTOEXEC.BAT file to download the fonts when you start your computer. If you want to manually download the fonts, select neither option. Select OK.

12. Select OK to return to the Printers dialog box.

13. Select Close to return to the Control Panel.

Now you can use the font in any Windows application. To display the associated screen font, install the FON file that was created using the techniques that you learned earlier in this appendix.

Changing Windows International Settings

Regardless of how you set up printers and fonts, Windows uses the default English-language character set for its display. However, because Windows has earned an international following, it also provides a way for users to customize the character set and keyboard layout, and how the date, time, and monetary figures are displayed.

If Windows is not already set up for the usages in your country, you can change these setting using the Control Panel. Follow these steps.

1. Select Control Panel from the Main group, and then select International. You will see the dialog box shown in Figure B.9.

2. Select your country from the Country drop-down list box. The settings for date, time, currency, and number formats will change automatically to match the usages in the country selected.

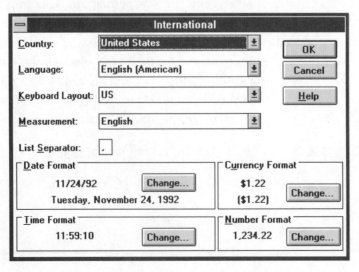

FIGURE B.9:

The International dialog box allows you to change settings to correspond to national usage.

3. Select a language and keyboard layout from the drop-down list boxes.

4. Select either English or Metric from the Measurement drop-down list box.

5. If any of the format settings are incorrect, select its Change command button.

A dialog box will appear, displaying alternate formats. Figure B.10, for example, displays the dialog box for changing the date formats. Choose your options, and then select OK to return to the International dialog box.

6. Select OK to return to the Control Panel.

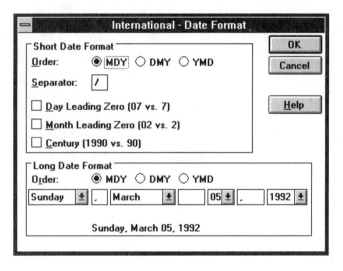

FIGURE B.10:

The International-Date Format dialog box is used for changing the date format.

INDEX

Help Yourself with Another Quality Sybex Book

Supercharging Windows
Judd Robbins

Here's a gold mine of answers to common questions, with details on undocumented features, optimization, and advanced capabilities. This book's wide-ranging topics include Windows for laptops, programming language interfacing, memory-resident software, and networking—just to name a few. Includes two disks full of productivity tools, utilities, games, and accessories.

1011pp; 71/2" x9"
ISBN: 0-89588-862-9

Available
at Better
Bookstores
Everywhere

Sybex Inc.
2021 Challenger Drive
Alameda, CA 94501
Telephone (800) 227-2346
Fax (510) 523-2373

SYBEX

Sybex. Help Yourself.

EASY DOS IT.

YOUR GUIDE TO DOS DOMINANCE.

SYBEX

FREE BROCHURE!

Complete this form today, and we'll send you a full-color brochure of Sybex bestsellers.

Please supply the name of the Sybex book purchased.

_____

How would you rate it?

_____ Excellent _____ Very Good _____ Average _____ Poor

Why did you select this particular book?

_____ Recommended to me by a friend

_____ Recommended to me by store personnel

_____ Saw an advertisement in _____

_____ Author's reputation

_____ Saw in Sybex catalog

_____ Required textbook

_____ Sybex reputation

_____ Read book review in _____

_____ In-store display

_____ Other _____

Where did you buy it?

_____ Bookstore

_____ Computer Store or Software Store

_____ Catalog (name: _____)

_____ Direct from Sybex

_____ Other: _____

Did you buy this book with your personal funds?

_____ Yes _____ No

About how many computer books do you buy each year?

_____ 1-3 _____ 3-5 _____ 5-7 _____ 7-9 _____ 10+

About how many Sybex books do you own?

_____ 1-3 _____ 3-5 _____ 5-7 _____ 7-9 _____ 10+

Please indicate your level of experience with the software covered in this book:

_____ Beginner _____ Intermediate _____ Advanced

Which types of software packages do you use regularly?

_____ Accounting _____ Databases _____ Networks

_____ Amiga _____ Desktop Publishing _____ Operating Systems

_____ Apple/Mac _____ File Utilities _____ Spreadsheets

_____ CAD _____ Money Management _____ Word Processing

_____ Communications _____ Languages _____ Other _____

(please specify)

Which of the following best describes your job title?

_____ Administrative/Secretarial   _____ President/CEO

_____ Director   _____ Manager/Supervisor

_____ Engineer/Technician   _____ Other _____
                                                    (please specify)

Comments on the weaknesses/strengths of this book: _____

_____

_____

_____

_____

_____

Name _____

Street _____

City/State/Zip _____

Phone _____

PLEASE FOLD, SEAL, AND MAIL TO SYBEX

SYBEX, INC.
Department M
2021 CHALLENGER DR.
ALAMEDA, CALIFORNIA USA
94501

SYBEX

SEAL

PROGRAM MANAGER KEYSTROKES

Keystroke	Function
Alt or F10	Activates the Menu bar.
Alt-Backspace	Undo the last editing action.
Alt-Esc	Switches to the next running or minimized application.
Alt-F4	Closes an application window.
Alt-Hyphen	Opens the Control menu of the active document window.
Alt-Print Screen	Copies the image of the active window to the Clipboard.
Alt-Spacebar	Opens the Control menu of the active application window.
Alt-Tab	Switches to open applications.
Ctrl-Esc	Displays the Task List.
Ctrl-F4	Closes a document window.
Ctrl-F6	Moves between group windows and icons.
Ctrl-Ins	Copies the selected text into the Clipboard.
Ctrl-Tab	Moves between group windows and icons.
Enter	Executes the application indicated by the selected icon in a group window.
Esc	Cancels the Menu bar
F1	Displays the Help Contents window.
Print Screen	Copies the screen image to the Clipboard.
Shift-F1	Context-sensitive help.
Shift-F4	Tiles windows side-by-side.
Shift-F5	Cascades windows.

DIALOG BOX KEYSTROKES

Keystroke	Function
Alt-key	Moves to, and toggles, dialog box option with the underlined character key.
Alt-↓	Pulls down a drop-down list.
Backspace	Deletes the character to the left of the insertion point, or deletes all selected text.